The Talk

Helping Your Kids Navigate Sex in the Real World

ALICE DREGER, PHD

ISBN: 1535188014
ISBN 13: 9781535188012

CONTENTS

ACKNOWLEDGMENTS

The author wishes to thank, at Kindle Singles, Carly Hoffmann for editing this work, David Blum for arranging the project, and Leah Zibulsky for copy-editing. She is also grateful to her husband and son for their help with this book; her literary agent, Betsy Lerner, for her excellent advice and support; her friend Dan Savage for many years of adult sex education; and her friend Ann Graham Nichols for reading a draft. She also thanks all of the people who have shared their life experiences with her over the past twenty-five years.

BIOGRAPHY

Alice Dreger, Ph.D., is a historian of sexuality and an award-winning writer. Her books include *Hermaphrodites and the Medical Invention of Sex*; *One of Us: Conjoined Twins and the Future of Normal*; and most recently, *Galileo's Middle Finger: Heretics, Activists, and One Scholar's Search for Justice*, named an Editors' Choice by *The New York Times Book Review*. Her writing about gender and sexuality has appeared in many national and international newspapers and magazines, including *WIRED*, *The Atlantic*, *Pacific Standard*, *The New York Times*, the *Los Angeles Times*, *The Wall Street Journal*, *New Statesman*, *The Guardian*, and *Slate*. Dreger is well known for her international advocacy on behalf of sexual minorities; her service in that area includes being the president and director of medical education for the Intersex Society of North America, advising the International Olympic Committee on sex testing in sports, and producing medical educational materials for the Association of American Medical Colleges. Her TED talk, "Is Anatomy Destiny?," has been viewed about a million times. She has been faculty at a number of universities, including most recently at Northwestern University's Feinberg School of Medicine program in Medical Humanities and Bioethics. Dreger has appeared on many broadcast programs around the world, including *The Oprah Winfrey Show*, NPR's *All Things Considered*, *Good Morning America*, and *CNN*, and has been a guest expert on Dan Savage's *Savage Lovecast*. In 2015, her live-tweeting of her son's abstinence sex-ed class went viral, causing international discussion about sex ed. For this, Dreger received an Outstanding Leadership Award in Comprehensive Sexuality Education from a national association that includes Planned Parenthood, GLSEN (the Gay, Lesbian, Straight Education Network), and the Healthy Teen Network. She lives in East Lansing, Michigan, with her family. Her website, which includes links to her media appearances and a list of her speaking appearances, is alicedreger.com, and her Twitter handle is @alicedreger.

Part 1

INTRODUCTION: BEING HONEST ABOUT SEX

One evening, when our son was three years old, he wandered into the bathroom after me, as kids are prone to do at that age. We had just wrapped up a party with friends at our house, and I was tipsy. Seeing me sit down on the toilet to pee, my son cocked his head and asked me in an adorably sympathetic voice:

"Does it make you *sad* that you don't have a penis?"

"No, honey," I answered without hesitation. "I *do* have one. It's on your father, and that's where I like it."

My husband screamed at me from the next room that I was going to cost us a fortune in psychotherapy.

I have a problem with honesty. I overuse it. Even when I'm sober.

One morning, when he was four and I had my period, my son saw some blood on the paper in the toilet. He asked me with some degree of concern what was going on, so I explained calmly to him that I was menstruating. I then answered his flood of questions about what exactly that meant.

Consequently, when I dropped him off at preschool a half hour later, and his teacher asked, "How are you and your mom today?" he answered, "I'm fine, but my mother is menstruating, so her uterine lining is sloughing."

As he went off to play at the sand table, his preschool teacher laughed about it. By then, she was used to his advanced knowledge of the human body. She reminded me of the time that the class was talking about baby cows and one child asked how the cow gets out of the mother's "tummy." The teachers temporarily froze, unsure of what to say. Finally, one realized how she could answer without using a word parents might object to their preschoolers knowing:

"Through the *birth canal*."

My son apparently raised his hand and asked if "the birth canal" was another name for "the vagina."

He then told the classmate who asked the question that the baby cow would be in the mother's *uterus*, not her stomach. If you were in your mother's stomach, he apparently explained quite authoritatively, you would be digested.

I have no idea what all the kids who had been told about babies in tummies thought at that point.

Children come programmed to be explorers. Starting even before they can hold up their heads, they spend a gigantic amount of energy every day poking at the world verbally and physically, trying to figure it out.

But when a child broaches any subject of sex—genitals, intercourse, pregnancy—we adults suddenly act as if that child is moving to climb up a slippery, fifty-foot ladder to a much-too-steep slide. We freak out, we pull the child back, and we suggest that that low-hanging tire swing would really be *much* more fun.

We might tell ourselves we steer kids away from sex talk for the children's sake. Sex and children are not supposed to go together—even if sexual intercourse is usually where children come from. Talking about sex with children feels inappropriate, not the responsible thing to do if you're an adult who takes their welfare seriously.

Besides, we adults know that while sex is a many-splendored thing, sex can often involve painful aspects—longing, shame, rejection, disappointment—and we try hard to keep children from getting hurt or even *knowing* about how much hurt lies ahead in life. Talking with them about sex feels like opening a door to a world of complicated emotions that children shouldn't have to feel.

But let's face it: We mostly avoid talking with kids about sex for our *own* sake. Talking about sex with kids makes *us* feel awkward and uncomfortable, even incompetent. How do you talk with a child about *sex?* Human sex acts are just bizarre! So are genitals. So are pregnancy, birth, and nursing.

I mean, if you really think about these things—try to look at them "objectively," as if you were an alien being just landed on Earth—you have to be, like, "What, now? Are you *serious?* Human mothers use modified sweat glands [that's what mammary glands are] to make food for their young, and the babies suck that stuff out of organs that are otherwise dressed up in *frilly lace* to be used as adult *sex objects? This* is how your species operates?"

It is really no wonder we try to talk about birds and bees instead of humans. It's no wonder that, the first time you tell a kid how the sperm usually gets to the egg, the child tends to react with some combo of disbelief and shock. (And so of course immediately asks you to repeat what just took all your strength to say.)

You might think that as your child gets older, it will get easier. Take my word for it—my baby boy is now 15 years old—it doesn't. As your children get older, they understand more and more about anatomy and adult social relations. Especially if you've been pretty open with them about the facts, they get better at asking challenging follow-up questions. As a consequence, talking to older kids about sex can feel even *more* awkward than talking to very young children, because older kids have a better sense of the gravity and the weirdness of it all. (Plus, they know they've been touching themselves…and they know we probably have been touching ourselves, too.)

So, bottom line: If you find yourself having a hard time talking with your little kid or your bigger kid about sex—if you find yourself having a hard time even *thinking* about talking with your kid about sex—you're a perfectly typical parent. The truth is, while I can joke about genitals with my adult friends as readily as any frat boy, the first time my kid cornered me and asked me *exactly how* his father's sperm reached my egg—he was five-and-a-half years old—I turned bright red, started stammering, and went into evasive maneuvers worthy of a fighter pilot in enemy territory. And I was a professional medical researcher who was in the midst of editing a book about parenting and sex development!

But we have to talk to our kids about sex. In fact, we have to be prepared to talk with them about sex *throughout their lives* as they develop. News flash: A single instance of "the talk" is not enough. As they grow, your children will *keep wanting* to know more and more about sex. They will *keep needing* to know more about sex. And they will *always deserve* to know more about sex than they can get from school, the playground, and the media.

If you find yourself thinking that talking to your kids about sex is overwhelming, try to remember that talking to your children calmly about sex is actually *protective.* Having regular, calm, honest talks with you about sex can keep your children safer from predators, help them know what to do if they get in trouble, and hopefully can help give them a better, more enjoyable sex life in the long run. And it might just keep *you* from being presented with grandchildren before your kids are ready to be parents. Conversing with your children about sex makes you a good parent, not a bad parent!

In the next part of this book, we're going to talk specifically about good parenting as well as the basics of how to communicate with your children. As I'll explain in more detail in the next part, what I'm recommending here about talking with children comes from my twenty years of experience in working professionally with families whose children were born with bodies that don't fit "normal" social expectations. Some of the parents I learned from had children born with intersex genitals (genitals that are in between male and female types). Some of them had had children who were born conjoined twins ("Siamese twins"). Some of them had children who were born with Down syndrome or cerebral palsy, or with a port wine stain (a purple-colored area of skin) on their face, or with a cleft lip. All of them had to deal with the rough parts of parenting—uncertainty, ambivalence, intense familial love, medical worries, and tough conversations—sooner than average.

Why did I have reason to learn about parenting from these people? My Ph.D. degree is in history of science, and I am especially interested in the history of anatomy. In graduate school, I took on studying the history of social and medical attitudes toward birth "defects," and so I ended up learning about a lot of families who had had children born with relatively unusual body types. Even though my son was born, five years into this work, with an average sort of body, I quickly realized that what I had learned from these extraordinary families could be applied to *any* parent-child relationship, including my own. That's because all parent-child relationships contain the same basic elements—fear, affection, ambivalence, delight, and so on—and no child is really "normal" in the sense of being predictably average in every way.

The main thing I learned from my work on parenting children with "different" bodies was this: Your children will do best if you don't spend a lot of time judging everything and everyone around you, because if you spend all your time judging everything and everyone around you, your children will feel constantly negatively judged by you and the rest of the world. Instead, you have to learn to talk with your children in ways that *describe* things and people around you. You have to get away from constantly engaging issues of shame and pride and instead just *be* together in the world, in constant, reality-based conversation.

Don't worry, I will explain much more in the next section about this approach to talking with your children about hard topics. In the sections after that, I will review what you should know about sexual anatomy and physiology, gender, sexual orientation and sexual practices. Ultimately, the basic method of instruction plus the nitty-gritty parts of this book should help you feel well educated and prepared going into these conversations with your children.

Okay, so let's start by talking about talking.

PART 2

THE SHAME-PRIDE AXIS AND HOW TO GET OFF OF IT

Give a man a fish and he'll eat for a day. Teach a man to talk to his children about sex, and he'll be able to answer when his children ask, "Daddy, why is that man trying to have sex with that fish?"

In all seriousness, there is no way I can anticipate and give you a scripted answer for every question your child might have about sex. Even if I had the space to do so, you wouldn't be able to memorize it all.

Instead, what I'm going to do here is to give you a *philosophy* of how to talk with your children about just about everything, including everything that's particularly hard to talk about—sex, death, family fights, cancer, what the hell has happened to the Republican Party since Abraham Lincoln was a member.

If you can get in the habit of following this approach to talking with your children, then you and they will find it easier to have meaningful, helpful conversations about many important topics, including sex.

But first, we need to cover some background on how your brain works as a parent.

You want your children to do well in the world. You want them to be well-liked, eventually loved by an excellent partner, successful in work, and happy. As a consequence, you are probably inclined to attempt constant course corrections in the flight paths that are your children's lives.

These course corrections start off innocuously. In public, you take your toddler's finger out of her nose and take her hand out of her pants. You teach your little boy how to use utensils and say "please" and "thank you." Then, as your children enter elementary school, you start fussing over their schoolwork, suggesting extracurricular activities, talking with them about what they will be when they grow up. You find yourself openly judging who among their peers makes a good friend or who could make a nice boyfriend or girlfriend. You praise your children when they do well by your standards—you announce your pride to your friends and family—and let your children know when they've gone off course.

The primary reason for all this—probably—is your child's long-term well-being. But there's also something in it for you: When your child does well, you look good, and you feel good. When they don't do well, you look bad, and you feel bad.

This feedback loop—involving your and your child's emerging identities in interplay with each other—results in the creation of something I've come to call "the shame-pride axis." This is an imaginary track that comes into existence slowly but surely in your parent-child world. Think of it as a measuring stick that runs from "very proud" to "very ashamed."

You will often find yourself doing whatever you have to do to pull your children toward the "very proud" end of the shame-pride axis: using time-outs for bad behavior; dressing them in stylish clothes; getting them braces, surgeries, or medications to make them look and act "better"; enrolling them in extra classes and sports; gently nudging them to set up international nonprofit foundations to help people in the developing world have cleaner hands, so that your brilliant children are featured on *CNN Heroes*.

You tell yourself that all this dragging of your child toward the "very proud" end of the axis is not for your sake. "My kid will be better off in the long run! She or he will save the world!" And you'll often be right about the benefits of your course corrections. It isn't just you who benefits. Your child and those around him or her often benefit.

Nevertheless, as they grow, most children find it increasingly exhausting to exist with you primarily on the shame-pride axis. Even when you indicate to them that you are terribly *proud* of them, they know that means they're *on that axis* where you might end up terribly *ashamed* of them if they slip up. They feel constantly judged by you and the world.

In their effort to please you, some children will push themselves very hard, judge themselves harshly, exhaust themselves, and finally come to dislike you. If the shame-pride axis is the only plane they've learned to live on with you, if they feel they cannot please you, your children will sometimes "prove" it by doing things they know will make you very ashamed.

While there's no question that children need you to sometimes do the yanking toward the pride end—it's part of your job in raising a child who will exist in civilized society—they really benefit from spending a lot of time with you *off* the shame-pride axis. The way you do this (and I'll explain this with various examples) is to listen to how you converse with your children and, as much as possible, move yourself from judging things to simply describing things. Think of it as shifting your role from being St. Peter at the gates of heaven—judging everyone and everything—to being a helpful local guide on a double-decker tourist bus.

I mentioned in the Introduction how I've spent the past twenty years learning from families with children who were born with socially challenging bodies. So let me refer to these families to explain more about what can happen if you communicate with each other mostly on (versus mostly off) the shame-pride axis:

As you might guess, in most cultures, children born with bodies that don't fit social expectations quickly become potential sources of shame for a family. So shame and pride immediately become vivid issues when a child is born "different." Through my research I came to notice that, when the parents in these cases spent their energy judging their children according to their culture's oppressive standards, their children typically did not do well. The parents who freaked out at their child's bodily difference and who stayed there, on the shame-pride axis, kept dragging their children to doctors or other specialists to be "fixed." Some of them actively hid their children so others would not see them.

The message these children got was clear: "You were born shameful." Even when they ended up, through interventions, with bodies that fit social norms for appearance and behavior, the children of these pride-obsessed parents often grew up feeling ashamed of themselves, upset with their parents, and generally depressed. Their low self-esteem sometimes also made them targets of sexual abusers.

By contrast, there were the parents who had decided that their children weren't born fundamentally "broken"—that some people just come different from the usual. Some of these parents were conservative religious people who had the belief "God doesn't make mistakes," and some were progressives with the belief that lots of what the world thinks is old-fashioned and needs changing. Regardless of the *reasons* for their more positive attitudes toward their children, these were all parents whose words and actions communicated the message "I can do what this child needs of me" (rather than "This child will have to change to meet my needs").

In *these* cases, instead of hiding and or trying to "fix" their children—instead of trying to move them from shame to pride—the parents helped their children see that the world could sometimes be unjust, mean, and stupid, but they did so by *describing* to their children the way the world works. They then signaled that they would just *be* in the world with their children the way their children *were*.

They didn't try to move their children to the "pride" side of the world's axis, nor did they become activists trying to push the world's pride toward their children. They pulled themselves and their children off that plane entirely and just lived together in peace. Often they did this because their children were expected not to live long, something that really gives you perspective about what matters in terms of your relationship with your children—something that frees you simply to love rather than to worry and judge.

I could see, in my studies, that the children who resulted from this kind of off-the-axis parenting turned out to be pretty strong, peaceful people. They had self-confidence and a kind of calm about them, but even more interestingly, they didn't go through the world frantically judging everybody and everything. They had good relationships with their parents—relationships of mutual respect that had clearly been established early. They were able to see social systems as things that could be ignored, challenged, or changed if they didn't work well. They didn't spend their whole lives feeling inadequate or trying to feel superior.

So how do *you* get off the shame-pride axis in interactions with your children? **Like the parents who did well with their born-different children, you consciously push yourself, in conversations with your child, to talk *descriptively* about the world *without judging* what you're talking about as good or bad. You favor *descriptive* talk over *normative* talk.** Here's one quick, everyday, made-up example to show you the difference.

Normative talk (judging, stuck on the shame-pride axis): "Your friend Jenny is so irresponsible, the way she jumps down the stairs and wants to climb on the roof! Her parents must be so out of control!"

Descriptive talk (describing, off the shame-pride axis): "We need to let Jenny know that, in our house, we don't go out on the roof or jump down the stairs, because doing those things can be fun, but they can result in serious harm. This is a safety rule in our house that everyone who visits our house follows."

It may sound like there is little difference here, but believe me, your child picks up the difference between mostly judging and mostly describing. In the judging talk above, your child hears that Jenny and her parents are awful people, and that by association, so is your child, because your child has chosen to be friends with Jenny. Your child also hears, in the judging talk, that Jenny's parents should be ashamed of themselves, and that by association, Jenny should be ashamed of her parents, who obviously don't love and protect her as much as you love and protect your child. As a consequence, your child is forced to choose between you and your love on the pride end, and Jenny and her family on the shame end. Her friendship with Jenny becomes a loyalty test administered by you.

By contrast, in the descriptive statement above, you're focused on what should actually matter: staying safe. There's no judging of Jenny or her parents or their household, and thus no loyalty test. Jumping down the stairs and going out on the roof aren't issues of shame and pride; you admit they can be fun but say they're primarily an issue of safety in your house, and everyone follows the rule to stay safe.

Let's look at another example. Imagine that in this case, your child has noticed that you don't see or talk about your father much, and she has noticed that this is different from the relationships she sees between other sets of parents and grandparents.

Normative (judging, on the shame-pride axis): "Grandpa was a horrible father to me. He was a self-centered, neglectful father most of the time, and mean and awful when he *was* paying attention to us."

Descriptive (describing, off the shame-pride axis): "My father was not around a lot for us. When he was around, he sometimes hit us or called us names."

Again, you may not notice the difference as being significant, but over time, your children will. Notice how in the normative statement, the child is getting the message you judge your father as having been a shameful, bad father. You're presenting yourself, by contrast, as a parent your child is supposed to be proud of. You're stuck on that shame-pride axis. I get that you're saying you want to be a better parent than your father was—signaling that you love your child—but you're also stuck on that axis of shame and pride where the child feels like parent-child relationships are primarily about judging each other.

In the descriptive statement, you're letting your child know that you didn't have such a good experience with your father. The focus in the descriptive talk about your father is less on shameful and prideful identities—pushing and pulling you and your father along the shame-pride axis—than simply on what your father did or didn't do as a parent. The focus is on *behavior,* which can be altered by a person, not *identity,* which we usually assume cannot be changed. Without heavy judgment language, the child understands that a parent who neglects, hits, and emotionally abuses his children is one who the child might not grow to love. Your child gets why you don't feel close to your father.

If you think about the conversations you've had with your child lately, or if you listen to yourself closely in the next two days, I would bet you can find instances where you are living on the shame-pride axis with your child. (Listen to how you talk about eating, friendships, schoolwork, etc.)

I know I could find instances from the past two days, easily—I am *sure* I don't go through *any* day of conversation with my son where I don't wander unnecessarily into normative talk. Again, we have to do *some* of that as parents: It's part of how we help children do well in civilized society. But much of the time we do it, we do it unconsciously to position ourselves as superior to others, and although it makes us feel superior and smug, it just ends up not really helping.

If you spend much of your time on the shame-pride axis with your children by using mostly judgmental talk, you might think you're helping them *do* well, but you may not be helping them *be* well. You're forcing them to live in a world where everything they do, say, or think is being judged by you, primarily as a source of potential pride or shame. And if you want them to come to you with their experiences, their concerns, their questions, then you are going to have to make clear to them that you're not going to spend the whole conversation judging everything along the shame-pride axis. People who judge you all the time are not people you go to with real questions and problems.

Starting from the time our son was a baby, we worked on following the basic approach I'm recommending here. Like all parents, we began to teach our child social norms early on—to not throw food or feces, to be kind and helpful to others, to not be violent. But we also tried to make sure he understood the world as much as possible through description rather than judgment, so that he did not feel that everyone (including him) was constantly on a stage to be judged by us, him, or others.

A lot of people watching us use this approach observed to us with surprise, "You talk to your child as if he is an adult!" That wasn't entirely the case; for example, you don't tell an adult about colors or letters or what sounds different animals make, and we did all that with our son, of course. But it *was* true that we tried to treat him respectfully and to focus on *describing* things and people and activities rather than judging everything like a panel at an Olympic figure-skating competition.

As he grew, we tried to signal to him in our descriptive language that people and social systems can vary and change, and we tried to let him know that there wasn't any question or topic that couldn't be raised with us. There was nothing that couldn't be described, discussed, and understood. We often found ourselves explaining to our young son how, to get what you'd like in the world, you have to figure out what each cultural experience requires of you. So, for example, we explained that in our house, he didn't have to eat anything he really didn't want to (we see this as part of respecting him as a person with the right to decide what to do with his body), but in most places he would be considered impolite and unfriendly if he did not eat at least a little of what is offered to him. We explained that in our house, he could throw a soft ball around with his friends, but he should ask permission if he wanted to do that in someone else's house. Descriptively explaining the social structures of the world empowered him; avoiding constant language of judgment helped him be more at ease in his explorations of himself and the world.

Perhaps because we were more attuned to parenting styles than average new parents, we often found ourselves watching what other parents did, and we noticed how children seemed to behave better—to be more calm, thoughtful, and confident—around parents who favored a descriptive approach over a normative approach. For example, when our son was a baby, we were seated on a long flight next to a mother with a preschooler. Her child was tired and frustrated at being stuck on the plane, and so she started to whine. Rather than saying, "Don't whine! You're so annoying when you whine!" the mother used descriptive language with a little fib: "When you speak in that very high voice, it is hard for me to hear you. Could you lower your voice and make it calmer so I can hear you better? Then we can talk with each other more easily." The child did so, and by the end of the flight, she was listening to herself and stopping herself from whining, not because her mother said it made her a bad child, but because her mother was more "able" to listen to her if her voice were lowered and made more calm.

When the flight attendant was slow to come after the mother pushed the call button, rather than saying, "What a bad flight attendant!" the mother said, "I think the flight attendant must be busy. Or maybe she just didn't hear the button. We'll ring the button again later if she doesn't come."

There were some parents at our son's schools who were especially good at shifting from language of judgment to language of description—from language that seemed to sort children into "good" and "bad" to language that seemed to appreciate variations among children. So when one preschool teacher said to a mother about her son, "His ability to pick up small objects at this young age is amazing!" and the mother saw another parent awkwardly standing next to her whose son was not so good (yet) at this task, the first mother said about her own son, descriptively, "He likes to build with Legos. They give you a lot of space for imagination." She shifted the talk from "My son is so great" to simply "My son has tastes that might be different, and that's fine."

One young teacher who had studied disability did a terrific teaching unit on it at our preschool. She brought in assistive devices—a wheelchair, a walker, and so on—and simply let the children talk about people they knew who used assistive devices. She then let them try them out. It was a way to simply say, "Some people have disabilities and they use assistive devices." There was no judgment involved (although some of the kids did start to brag about their grandparents' cool assistive devices!). The teacher didn't make people with disabilities out to be heroes or sad stories. It was just a description of the world in which people with disabilities were real and present. I remember that, shortly after this unit, my son was building a train station out of blocks with another boy when he blurted out, "We forgot the ramps!" Disability had become a more normal part of their vision through a simple descriptive lesson. They didn't have to feel ashamed of people in their families who happened to have or to develop disabilities.

When our son had sexuality-related questions, we tried as with everything to describe rather than judge. That's why, when as a preschooler he asked me about the blood on the toilet paper, I simply described menstruation rather than signaling that it was shameful by trying to change the subject. When he asked me if menstruation hurt, I just described the pain as being something like a charley horse in my uterus. I told him the contractions were similar to the ones I had when I gave birth to him, although, as I told him, menstrual contractions are a lot less intense.

When he was about four, our son came crying to me one day because his preschool friend George had told him that two men can't get married. He knew that our friends Brian and Steve were a couple, and so it upset him a lot that George seemed to be saying that Brian and Steve couldn't love each other the way my husband and I love each other. He saw this as George being "mean."

I sat our son down with the globe, and we talked about where on Earth (literally) Brian and Steve could get married legally, how legally being married and being in love are not at all the same thing, and how the world had changed in terms of treatment of gay people since a hundred years ago. I explained how for many years, women could not vote, and how that slowly changed across the world as most people decided that was unfair. I can vote, I told him, but my great-great-great-grandmother could not when she was alive. We talked about how odds were good that by the time our son was 25, gay marriage would be legal in the United States.

I could have gone into that conversation normatively rather than descriptively. I could have said, "George's parents are bigots if they have taught him that gay people can't love each other." While that might have made me feel smug, it wouldn't have helped my son understand what was going on around him—it wouldn't have helped him understand George was right about the law, but that marriage doesn't tell you who is in love—and it would likely have left him in a situation where he felt conflicted about George and maybe felt a loyalty test: George versus Steve and Brian. Instead, he went back to school the next day and explained to George the history that we had talked about, explaining how the world was changing. He explained that men *could* love each other, and women could love each other too, even if they weren't legally allowed to marry.

We used the same approach with children visiting our house who fondled themselves a lot—an awkward situation! We would say to them, "That's something people do in their own rooms, because touching ourselves in that way is something we do in private. Wait until you are in private to do that, please." This simple description told them what we needed them to know without imparting lots of heavy judgment that would signal that sexual feelings are strange or shameful. (By contrast, when my conservative Roman Catholic father caught me with my hands down my pants, he screamed at me that I was going to hell. I'll let you judge that one.)

My descriptive responses have always tended to be longer than my husband's—more than once we have been compared to Miss Piggy and Kermit the Frog in terms of our very different personalities—but we both have used the approach of trying to answer sex questions as we do other questions about bodies and behaviors. When our son was little and my husband and he were peeing into the toilet together, our son asked him, "How come your penis is always wrinkly but mine is smooth sometimes?" Me? I would have launched into a description of how erections work and what they're for later in life. But my husband simply replied, "Mine is smooth sometimes too." That was really all our son wanted to know at that time: that there was nothing odd about his penis sometimes being smooth. My husband's simple, calm, descriptive answer very much conveyed "You can ask me anything you want about your genitals or mine."

In parenting our son when he was young, we found it very useful to have a book given to us by an artist friend called *How It Works: The Human Body*, by Kate Barnes and Steve Weston. It's a children's "atlas of the human body" and had helpful pages showing and explaining the nervous system, the digestive system, the respiratory system, the reproductive system in males and females, and so on. In the section on reproduction, it had drawings of the male and female sex organs (although it didn't show the parts of the vulva, which I found frustrating; I had to show my son an adult anatomy book to show him a vulva). The child's atlas also provided drawings of human egg and sperm, a young fetus growing in its mother's womb, and a baby at full-term in the womb, ready for birth, with the umbilical cord still attached.

We pulled this book out every now and then and went over all of it— all of the body systems—and we would pause when we got to the pages about sexuality and reproduction, because it gave our son a chance to ask questions about that. Doing this in the context of this very descriptive book about the human body conveyed the message "This is just a natural part of your body." There were no more shame or pride issues about penises and uteruses than there were about livers and kidneys—that is to say, they were all just parts we could talk about.

That's not to say the book answered *all* his questions, even though it was pretty good about briefly mentioning erections, penile-vaginal intercourse, and male ejaculation. A book will never do it all. So, in spite of our use of the human atlas, when he was five and a half, he cornered me and wanted to know the real deal about intercourse.

I was *somewhat* psychologically prepared because that age, I had learned earlier from a smart mother, is actually a common one for children to have this question, even though parents often think they must be too young. There have now been a number of parents of five- and six-year-olds whose children are suddenly acting up for no apparent reason to whom I've said, "She/he probably wants to know about sexual intercourse"; in every case, when the parent has gotten up the gumption to ask the children if they want to talk about sex, the children have said yes, calmed down, and stopped acting up after an honest talk.

The sex talk I had with my kid at age five and a half happened on Christmas Eve. Our son had gotten too many great presents and was consequently overstimulated. By about nine in the evening, way past his normal bedtime, we sent him to his room to cry it out because he was generally being a pill. My husband, meanwhile, had dared to eat mussels brought by a neighbor, in spite of the fact that we knew he couldn't eat scallops or clams without digestive disaster. ("Mussels might be different," he told me hopefully, while downing about a dozen.) After forty-five minutes of listening to my son weep hysterically, and seeing my husband looking increasingly gray, I went up to my son's room.

"I can't stop crying!" he managed to say, somewhat alarmed, through his screaming tears. I calmly told him I understood. I said that I had cried like that sometimes in my life too. He asked me when I had ever cried like he was crying. I reminded him that I had had a miscarriage two years before I had him and told him it had made me so sad, I had cried like he was crying, because I really wanted a child.

He suddenly stopped crying, as if a switch had been flipped.

"Yeah," he said to me, like he was talking sports or the weather, "how *exactly* did Dad's sperm get to your egg?"

Flabbergasted, turning red, I said, "Uh, through his penis."

"But *how*," he pressed me, "did it get from his penis up into your womb?"

After hemming and hawing, I pulled out that atlas, explained erections to him, and said that they occur in adult men when they are sexually stimulated. I explained that before he was conceived, his father had had an erection and had put his penis into my vagina, because that's what penis-vagina sexual intercourse is, and that he had had an ejaculation that put the semen in me. He was aghast. Really? he asked. Really, I said. That's how sex between a man and a woman usually works, and that can lead to a baby.

Ejaculations, I explained, happen when you're a grown man and you reach a high point in sex called a climax or an orgasm. The prostate (I pointed to the picture) plus the testes (pointed again) make semen, and the semen comes out of the tip of the penis, where pee usually comes out. One of the sperm in his dad's semen, I explained, met one of my eggs that time, and so he was conceived. I told him it was a few weeks later when I figured out I was pregnant.

My son asked me a bunch of follow-up questions. He was now completely calm—calm enough to ask me, "How come you are all red and having trouble talking?"

I told him that adult sex was a pretty intense experience—that's why adults refer to it all the time, because it's intense—and so it made adults kind of awkward when we talk about it with children. I assured him he should ask me anyway, because I could handle it. When we were done, he laid down happily to go to sleep. I went down to check on my husband, who wanted to know what on earth had happened to shift the kid from hysterical weeping to calm conversation. (He had heard the crying suddenly stop.) I told him. My husband expressed as much surprise as I had felt, thanked me for explaining sexual intercourse to our kid, and promptly threw up all the mussels. That was a Christmas Eve to remember.

Our son was a bit unusual for a boy in asking so bluntly about sex at that age. But with a daughter, it would not be all that unusual for her to ask you about sex when she's about five years old. Parents who have both sons and daughters will tell you that they are much more likely to get into sex talks with their daughters than their sons. This is probably because, the world over, parents worry more about their daughters' sexual lives than their sons', since their daughters are at greater risk for sexual abuse and sexual assault. They are also, um, at much greater risk of pregnancy than sons. But a gender difference in parent-child sex talk probably also exists because, developmentally, girls are on average more socially aware and more articulate than boys the same age. So girls are simply more likely to start these conversations.

That said, with both sons and daughters, there are far more opportunities available for sex talk than you will realize if you're thinking there is one Talk. Our son was about seven or eight years old when I found an opportunity to explain to him that abortion is the name for when a doctor helps a woman end a pregnancy. He had heard people talking about it on the radio, and although he didn't ask me outright what abortion was, I could see by the look on his face he really wanted to know. So I asked him: "Do you want to know what abortion is?" He answered yes.

As with all else, I explained abortion descriptively in simple terms; I explained that doctors use either a drug that causes something like a miscarriage or use surgery to take out the fetus along with the amniotic sac. I explained that either way, the fetus dies—that that is the goal, to end the pregnancy without a baby.

He was shocked to learn that women sometimes purposefully kill fetuses by ending pregnancies (culture aims to expose children only to Hallmark versions of babies and parenthood), but we dealt with this by again talking about it descriptively—how most abortions involve only tiny embryos, why a woman might feel she had to make that choice, and why it could be a very hard choice for some women, especially later in pregnancy. Sometimes describing the world requires describing things that will shock your child, and even shock you as you describe it. (I felt a little disoriented talking about this with the child who had been in my womb.) So it's always a good idea in that case to ask follow-up questions of your child, like, "Does it make sense to you? How does it make you feel?" You should revisit the conversation and the questions the next day if the conversation got very intense. (Children will often want to talk more but will be unsure how to start.)

It is also fine, in such a conversation, to describe how *you* feel about something and to describe why you feel that way, using the first-person *I*. And it's not a bad idea to describe how people who differ from you feel and to try to describe with reasonable sympathy why they feel that way. I descriptively explained to my son during our abortion talk why I am pro-choice and why my parents are not. It helped him see our different world-views and also to understand why abortion is still such a heavy political and moral debating point.

As our son has grown, we have made a point of teaching him more and more names for sex-related things. We moved on, from preschool to elementary school, to explaining that "smooth penis" is called an erection and that touching yourself in your genital area for pleasure is common and is called masturbation. Because we laid down a good foundation for talking about sex when he was little, by the time he was a teenager, we could *usually* pretty comfortably talk about sex. So, he could come home and tell me with comfort what was going on in his sex-ed class and what he thought of the misinformation being distributed in the name of "absti-nence education." I remember one time when he was about 13 when his father and I started telling him some of the funny expressions people have for masturbation. We were all cracking up, but the message we were con-veying was clear: Masturbation is common, sex is a normal part of adult life, and we can talk about it without fear.

By the way, if you're feeling like you're late coming to this book be-cause your child is already a teenager, consider being honest and explain-ing to him or her that you've read this book and want to try talking more together about sex. It is never too late to shift your conversation, especially if you're honest with your children about what's what.

And take it from me: Talking with your children primarily in the de-scriptive mode rather than the judging mode is a really fascinating habit, because not only does it signal to your children that it's okay to ask you about *anything*, and not only does it signal that you trust them to act and think in a relatively mature fashion (and, believe me, they rise to that!), it also frees you from feeling like you have to constantly work at being some kind of world leader in the parenting department. It means you can just sit on the floor and really talk with them, because you're not whacking away at the world with a big judging sword all the time. It also lets you into their world instead of constantly dragging them into ours, because they feel *they can describe things to you* without fear you will judge them. It lets them build a world of their own, where they don't feel the need to agree with you in order to have your love and respect. It's kind of magical.

I'm not going to pretend that this is always easy! Personally, I struggled over how to talk to my young son about childhood sexual abuse without giving him the message that touching your genitals is a bad thing or that his doctor is a pervert. What I ended up telling him was this: Sometimes we touch our genitals because we are dealing with bodily needs—peeing and pooping, for example. Sometimes we touch them because it feels good. Sometimes a doctor touches them to check on our health. When you're not yet sexually mature—before you hit puberty and grow into an adult—these are the only reasons an adult should touch your genitals: to help you with bodily needs and health. If an adult tries to touch your genitals for other reasons, or wants you to touch theirs, that's not okay because that's not something for children. It's like how young children should not be offered cigarettes or race cars to test-drive. That is stuff for adults. If that happens, please tell me or Dad right away, and we'll help you with it. And always tell us if anyone does anything that makes you feel weird or unsafe so we can talk about it.

I also found it really hard to figure out how to talk to our 11-year-old son about online pornography that he might encounter as he started being online a lot. In circumstances like this, where you can't figure out how to talk to your kid about something sexual, it isn't a bad idea to retreat to your corner and talk it over with another adult to figure out what to say. You could even practice on the other adult.

In this case, I asked my husband what we should say, and we decided after some discussion that he should do the talking on this one. I sat in and mostly kept my mouth shut. He explained to our son why pornography is so common—because when sex is done right, it is pleasurable, so adults seek it out in different ways. He also explained that a lot of pornography is unrealistic; the men's penises are often larger than average, the women's genitals often have no hair even though women naturally grow pubic hair, and often people who seem to be strangers are having sex, which is in fact pretty uncommon in most people's lives. He told our son he thought it was best to learn about sexual intercourse mostly through his own lived experiences, so that he has a realistic understanding of sex and finds out for himself what feels good or not good.

He further said that if something online makes him uncomfortable, it's a good idea to step away, and talk with us about it if that helps. I reminded our son that if a friend was pushing him to watch pornography and he felt uncomfortable with it, he could do what I taught him to do if a friend pulled out his parent's gun "to play with it"—say, "I forgot I have a dentist appointment! I have to go!" and head home immediately without losing face. (And if it's a gun, definitely tell us so we can talk to that parent about a gun being "played with.")

There is no question that there are times you need to impart values and judgments to your child. It's how you teach morality, which young children especially do need to be taught. For us, that has meant teaching our child the value of the Golden Rule (treat others as you wish to be treated) and especially of being helpful to others. Besides, when you are doing things like conveying the message that sexual touching requires consent, you're obviously conveying values and judgments.

And for some sexual topics, you really have to lay down clear good or bad judgments. For example, it's really important to tell your children that if any adult says to them, "Don't tell your parent(s) about this," that's not okay, and they need to tell you about it as soon as they are back with you, even if it is Grandma telling them not to tell you about a surprise present she's getting you. You also need to teach them in no uncertain terms to tell you if they feel physically or emotionally unsafe in any way and that it is not okay for people to make them do things with their body that don't feel safe. Sometimes that means offending or inconveniencing another adult who wants to touch your child—Auntie Marge wants a hug and kisses!— but I think in the long run, this is the best approach to teaching respect for oneself and others.

There may be times you do need to let your child know you are ashamed of him or her. For us, this occurred especially when our son was little and still learning the Golden Rule. If he treated someone else badly, we told him that we were very unhappy with that and sent him into a "time-out." But we strictly reserved the message "This is shameful—you are making me ashamed of you" for violations of the Golden Rule.

There are also times when you need to let your child know unequivocally that you are proud of her or him. This is necessary, for example, when the world is making your child feel ashamed for stupid reasons. So, if your teenager is gay or transgender and has the courage to come out to you about it, it makes sense to say, "I am so proud of you for having the courage you do about this!" Attending a pride parade with your child in such a circumstance makes total sense, because you're going to need to fight against the "You should be ashamed of yourself" barrage of messages a person gets, still, in the world if that person is gay or transgender.

In short, there will be times when you must convey judgment of shame or pride, or convey messages about what is good and bad in the world. That's *necessary*. But it's a good idea to take the time, whenever parenthood allows for it, to think about the messages you're giving your child in ordinary conversation, including in *how* you speak about things. Leaning, whenever possible, toward describing rather than judging—getting off the shame-pride axis—will set up a style of communication between you and your child that conveys to her or him the importance of knowledge, careful thought, and trying to understand the people and systems around you. Talking in the descriptive mode will help your child learn to describe to people how she or he is feeling, which is really important when your child grows to the point of consensual sexual relations.

I think you'll also find, as I have, that talking to your kids about sexual anatomy and physiology, gender, sexual behaviors, sexual orientations, etc., is a lot *easier for you* when you realize you just have to describe, in as accessible terms as possible, what's what. Thinking "How do I describe this to this child?" takes you back to basics, and takes away some of the freak-out feeling that may occur when you find yourself talking with your child about sex, where you're worried about trying to impart everything about right and wrong about sex in a short conversation.

Keep in mind that *children forget almost everything*—although never what you wish they'd forget (like the time I slammed my son's tiny fingers in an airplane bathroom door by accident). So you might think you've had "the talk" when it comes to sex, but the truth is you have to *keep* talking about sex, throughout their childhood and young adulthood, because they won't get it all, and a lot of what they get, they will forget.

You also can't wait forever for your child to bring up sexual questions. The world will soon give him or her the message "It's not okay to ask anyone about sex!" so you have to work past that. Look for logical opportunities to talk about body parts and about sex. If you're with your child and something happens around you that implicates sex—maybe it's a very sexual advertisement, or a couple making out on a park bench, or two dogs humping, or an older relative talking about someone "living in sin"—sit down as soon as possible with your child and use that as a reason to talk about sex. Do not assume your child didn't notice; *children notice everything*, and they feel much calmer and happier when someone they trust is willing to help them unpack strange and stressful things they are seeing and hearing in the world.

This doesn't mean you have to talk about sex every time you see it around you. (In our culture, you'd have no time to discuss anything *but* sex.) But try to see what your child is seeing and hearing, and try to help when something might be confusing, unclear, or scary. Again, if you do this with everything else too—neighborhood fights, the death of a pet or other loved one, a relative's cancer diagnosis—then you're setting up a healthy context in which you treat sex as a normal part of our world that we can talk about without fear. It's just one more part of life.

PART 3

THE BASICS OF SEX ANATOMY AND PHYSIOLOGY

If you're going to talk to your kid about sex, you will need to know the basics. In this section, I'm going to give you a review of the basics of human sex anatomy and physiology. In the next part, I'll give you the basics of gender, and then in the next part, the basics of sexual feelings and behavior. In giving you these reviews of the basics, I am figuring maybe you haven't spent the past several decades, as I have, studying this stuff. Besides, if your own school's sex ed was anything like the average in America, you probably got some combo of wrong and inadequate information where sex is concerned. Bonus: Pass all this secret wisdom on to your child and, like me, you can have a preschooler who says to people, "*Most* boys have a penis and a scrotum and *most* girls have a clitoris and a vagina."

In this section, the word *sex* is mostly going to refer to our sexual anatomy (parts) and physiology (functioning). This will include information on our sex chromosomes, genitals, gonads (ovaries and testes), and what we call the secondary sex characteristics. Secondary sex characteristics are those noticeable anatomical changes that happen to our body at puberty; besides pubic and armpit hair, secondary sex characteristics include rounded breasts and hips in women, and, in men, beards and mustaches, relatively prominent Adam's apples, and distinctive musculature.

As you have probably noticed, humans naturally come in two sex types. As you may not have heard, they also come in a whole bunch of other types most people don't talk about. We'll get to that in a bit. First, an important bottom line: *Sex development is complicated*...which is exactly the reason that nontypical sex development (including intersex) sometimes happens. But we can all understand the basics, especially if someone helps us review it a few times in a nonjudgmental fashion.

A biological mother's egg has about half the genetic material that will eventually make a child, and the biological father's sperm has the other half. (I'm specifying "biological" here simply to recognize that many children have one or more parents who were not their biological parents.) The egg and sperm usually contribute 23 chromosomes each to the future-child.

Usually, among the 23 chromosomes, the egg carries one X chromosome. Usually, among the 23 chromosomes, the sperm carries either an X or a Y chromosome. If an egg with its one X mashes up with a sperm with one X, usually that XX combo will lead to development of a female child (XX with a total of 46 chromosomes—something scientists and doctors refer to as 46, XX). If an egg with its one X mashes up with a sperm with one Y, usually that XY combo will lead to development of a male child (XY with a total of 46 chromosomes, or 46, XY). So:

- 23 chromosomes including X from the egg + 23 chromosomes including X from the sperm = 46, XX offspring, which usually develops as a typical female
- 23 chromosomes including X from the egg + 23 chromosomes including Y from the sperm = 46, XY offspring, which usually develops as a typical male

Odds are high that you are either a 46, XX female or 46, XY male, although odds are also high you've never had a chromosomal test, so you're just assuming you know what you have. (That's fine. I'm just assuming I know what I have, because like most people, I've had no reason to check.)

For the first few weeks after an egg and a sperm successfully merge in the act we call conception, XX and XY embryos have the same starter sex parts. In other words, we all started, very early in human development, with the same kinds of cells, whether we are 46, XX or 46, XY. But somewhere around the seventh week after conception, XX and XY embryos start to *sex-differentiate*. That means that, starting at that time, those starter sex parts usually take only one of two routes, with XX going toward a female body type and XY going toward a male body type.

Scientists have figured out that the reason this happens is because of a gene usually on the Y chromosome, called the SRY gene. If an embryo has an SRY gene in its chromosomes, then that gene sends instructions to turn those starter parts male. So, if there's an SRY gene, the gonads in the developing embryo will become testes instead of ovaries. This will cause a relatively high level of testosterone in the developing embryo and then the developing fetus, which, if everything is working the usual way, will cause the external genitals to form as the male type.

If the SRY gene isn't there, then the gonads in the developing embryo are told by the genes to turn those gonads into ovaries. The resulting relatively low level of testosterone usually means that the external genitals will form as the female type in the developing fetus.

So it's not really the Y chromosome that determines which way an embryo will usually develop in terms of sex but the SRY gene on the Y chromosome. Have it, usually you'll become male. Lack it, usually you'll become female.

As you probably already know, in terms of a phallic organ (the main sexual organ related to sexual pleasure), the typical female will be born with a clitoris, and the typical male will be born with a penis. The clitoris and the penis are actually the same organ developmentally. Whether an embryonic phallus ultimately turns into a clitoris or penis depends in large part on how much testosterone is in the developing fetus. More testosterone in the developing fetus, it will grow a penis. Less, it will grow a clitoris.

Both the clitoris and the penis are packed with highly sensitive nerves, although in the nerve-packing department, the clitoris wins, hands down. (See what I did there?) The clitoris is, centimeter for centimeter, vastly more sensitive than the penis. By the way, the fact that the clitoris and penis are the same organ, developmentally speaking, is why the clitoris is so important to orgasm for adult females. Most women need it to be touched to reach orgasm. (Guys: *You* try reaching orgasm without touching your phallus. Good luck!) We'll talk more about orgasms when we talk about sexual feelings and behaviors in Part 5.

Both the penis and the clitoris have extensions that go down deeper into the body, which you can kind of feel if you do a good self-exam with your fingers. (It's fine to take a mirror and examine your genitals to understand them better.) Most of the clitoris is actually on the *inside* of the body, beyond where you can feel it from the outside. The bit of the clitoris you can touch with the finger is really just the tip of the volcano. We'll talk more about that, too, when we talk about sexuality. A fair chunk of the penis is also inside the body, anchored down.

The clitoris and the penis both come at birth with a foreskin, which is a little flap of extra skin that covers the top part when the organ isn't erect. (Clitorises, like penises, can become erect, by filling with blood, when the owner is sexually excited.) Foreskins are highly sensitive tissues, and studies suggest that in many females, the clitoral foreskin is important to touch to reach orgasm. Although the foreskin is perfectly natural in both males and females, some people decide for various reasons to cut off the foreskin of baby boys. That's called circumcision. I happen to think it is a bad idea to cut off any healthy, living tissue, especially if it is sexual tissue, unless the person being cut has consented or there's a serious medical problem going on, but you'll have to forgive me for not getting deep into the circumcision debate here. (You will find a theme in this book that teaching your child to be sexually responsible requires you to repeatedly signal your respect for her or his body.)

The typical female has labia majora (that's Latin for "big lips"), the fleshy pillows on either side of the vaginal opening. The typical male has a scrotum. Just as the penis and the clitoris start out as the same organ early in development, the labia majora and the scrotum are the same organ, developmentally speaking. Females also have labia minora ("little lips") around the clitoris. All of these organs have a lot of nerves too.

Listen carefully to me on the following, so I don't have to yell at you if we ever meet and start talking about genitals: *Vulva—not vagina—is the correct term for the female's outside package.* The vagina is only the name for the tube that runs from the outside of the female up to her womb. The vulva, which, again, is external, includes the labia majora and minora, the clitoris, and the opening (introitus) of the vagina.

So far as I can ascertain, *junk* is the correct term for the male's outside package. Medicine should probably come up with a fancier name for it so boys don't feel left out and so they recognize the difference between the vagina and the vulva.

The typical female is born with two ovaries in her lower abdomen, and the typical male has two testes, usually in his scrotum when he is born, although some testes can take a while to descend from the abdomen into the scrotum. (Having testes stay too long in the abdomen can be a medical concern, so that's why your son's pediatrician will check, during regular exams, to see if his testes have descended.) As I mentioned earlier, the testes and ovaries start out as the same organs but differentiate because of the presence (in males) or absence (in females) of the SRY gene.

While males and females share many, many sex organs developmentally speaking, there are some internal sex organs that will usually develop only in the male or only in the female. Those happen because of lots of complicated biochemical signaling during prenatal development.

As far as internal differences, the female fetus will usually develop a vagina. The vagina is a strong, muscular, flexible tube that will run from her outside genitals (her vulva) up to her uterus. There's nothing in the male like this. The cervix is the lower part of the uterus, where it connects to the vagina. The male fetus usually develops a prostate, which will later make the juice his sperm will swim in. There's nothing in the female like the prostate. A man's ejaculate is basically a smoothie made up of prostate juice plus sperm from the testicles. There are other important internal differences between males and females in terms of parts and hormones, but the chief ones to know about are the vagina and the prostate, as those organs matter a lot to people's sexual experiences.

I once became good friends with a 28-year-old woman, well into double digits in terms of number of male sex partners, who didn't know the following, so forgive me if you already know this:

Men have two holes "down there," whereas women have three.

Men have a pee hole (in medicine, called a urinary meatus), usually at the tip of their penises, plus an anus, where the poop comes out.

Women have a pee hole toward the front of their genitals, near the base of the clitoris. Roughly at the midpoint of the crotch, between a woman's legs, is the opening to her vagina. And bringing up the rear, so to speak, is her anus. (No, I don't know which one of her holes my friend didn't know about before she met me. I couldn't ask because I had trouble getting my jaw off the floor.)

Babies' genitals often look kind of funny to adults because they are immature. I mean the baby's genitals are immature, although we adults are often immature about genitals.

Baby boys' penises are much smaller compared to the rest of the body than they typically will be after puberty, because pubertal hormones make the penis grow disproportionately more than the rest of the body. Baby boys also often have large "fat pads" on their lower abdomens that can make their penises look quite small. Parents who haven't seen baby's penises often are surprised at how small their sons' penises look. Penis size at birth, by the way, is not well correlated with adult penis size. Translation: How small or big a baby's penis is won't tell you how small or big his penis will be when he's fully grown.

Baby girls' clitorises and labia are sometimes swollen from birth (everything gets squished around, especially during a vaginal birth), so they will sometimes appear large or will appear to shrink back in the days after birth.

No matter what porn will have you believe, genital sizes and shapes actually vary *a lot*, as much as ears and noses and jawlines and lips. Girls can have clitorises that look fairly big, and they can be born with their labia somewhat stuck together. Boys can be born with small penises and have the pee hole somewhere other than the very tip of the penis. (Having the pee hole somewhere other than the tip of the penis is actually pretty common; it's called hypospadias and is estimated to occur in 1 in 150 male births.) It's also common for baby boys' testicles not to be fully descended. All of this means that a lot of babies don't have genitals that look like the "typical" baby boy's or girl's.

When a child has genitals that have formed in the womb to be *very much in between* the male and female types, we usually call this an intersex condition or a difference of sex development (DSD). If your child has genitals that look different from the typical in any way, you should talk to your pediatrician about whether there might be some underlying medical concerns. Most genital variation is benign—that means it might look different, but the difference is totally harmless. But some types of genital variation can signal an underlying health problem that requires treatment for your child's health. (Try not to confuse looking different, or having a different-than-typical kind of function, with being *unhealthy*. Genitals that look different but work fine don't need surgery, and genital surgery risks function, including sexual sensation. You don't want your child to have genital surgery unless she or he really needs it for dire health reasons.)

Genitals are one place DSD or intersex development can show up. But because sex biology also includes chromosomes, internal organs, and hormones, people can vary from the sexually typical in lots of ways *besides* genitals. Sometimes differences of sex development aren't detected until puberty, or until someone thinks she or he is infertile, and sometimes they're never found out, because there's just no reason to look closely. If we add up all the ways sex can vary, about one in a hundred people are born with some kind of difference of sex development (different from typical male or typical female).

Some people are born with sex-chromosome variations. So they may be born with 46, X (Turner syndrome) or 47, XXY (Klinefelter syndrome). Some people are born with a mix of sex-chromosome types, so that some of their cells have, say, 46, XX and some have 46, XY. Some people are born with 46, XX like most females, but they have an SRY gene like most males, and in that case, their development will head mostly down the male pathway. Some people are born with 46, XY (typical male chromosomes) but lack the genes to develop cellular receptors for testosterone; in that case, their bodies will head developmentally mostly down the female pathway, so much so that they often won't find out they have 46, XY until at least late puberty.

You can be born looking totally typically male or totally typically female but have nontypical sex development *inside*. You can also be born looking intersex in terms of your genitals but be totally typically male or totally typically female in every other way.

You also can be born missing sex parts outside or inside. You can have some combo of male and female parts outside or inside. You can even be born with duplication of sex organs, although that is rarer. Because I study intersex and work for the rights of people born with differences of sex development, I know one woman who was born with two uteruses, and so she refers to her "hysterectomies," plural. (She also had three kidneys, which is less uncommon.) I've met a number of men born with one testicle, and one born with three. You may have heard news stories of the porn star born with two penises. He is not the first man in history to be born with that double whammy.

Sex development is way, way more fascinating than they told you in school, if they told you anything. I think of human sex development as being like when I go bowling: Most of the time, my ball is going to either go in the left gutter (male) or the right gutter (female). But about 1 out of 100 times, the ball might go down the middle and leave something like a 7-4 split—something much more interesting than the gutter balls that are typical male and typical female sex development.

If your child's sex development is not going as you expected at any point, it's a good idea to check in with your pediatrician to make sure there are no medical concerns at play. And if it turns out your child does have a difference of sex development or an intersex condition, don't panic. As I've already explained, we now realize it actually happens to lots of people, and if you handle it calmly and recognize that lots of unexpected things happen in parenting, you and your child can be fine with it, even if it means that your child needs some medical care or help later in life with infertility or some other concern.

Okay, now let's talk some more about sexual physiology—how our sexual anatomy *functions*.

Erections of phallic organs (penises and clitorises and everything in between) happen in pretty much everyone, although because the external clitoris is small, its erection is typically less visible than a penis's erection. From babyhood on, boys will sometimes have quite visible erections. If you come upon an erection when you're changing your newborn baby's diaper, you should not yell for your physician-husband, as I did, with alarm: "Come quick! The baby's penis is all swollen!" You will just be embarrassed that he has to remind you what an erection is.

Incidentally, it is common for babies and young children to touch and play with everything on their bodies, but they may touch their genitals more than the rest because, let's face it, touching yourself there can feel pretty damned interesting. Even *good*. Little kids don't have adult sexuality, but they do have nerves down there that will grow up to become the nerves that are at the basis of this book. They figure out early on that touching there can feel good. Again, a good way to address masturbation in children is just to say, "Touching ourselves that way is something we do in private. Please do it when you are alone."

When we hit puberty, biochemical signaling ("It's time!") causes our ovaries or testes to ramp up the production of sex hormones. This ramp-up leads to development of those secondary sex characteristics—the features that make us look like mature men and women. It also leads to the development of acne, as well as the realization that your parents are deeply tiresome.

Because of a hormonal surge from the testes at puberty, boys' Adam's apples and penises usually grow bigger, their bodies get hairier, their voices drop, and they develop musculature that makes them look, well, more manly. Because of a hormonal surge from the ovaries at puberty, usually girls start menstruating, their bodies get hairier, their voices mature, and they develop breasts and rounder hips, and so they look, well, more womanly.

Males and females actually all make the same *types* of sex hormones (men make some estrogen; women make some testosterone), but the different relative *levels* of sex hormones determine how you will develop, including in terms of which type of puberty you will go through.

As already mentioned, after pubertal development sets in, females typically start to menstruate. Although twenty-eight days is the average female menstrual cycle, some girls and women have shorter or longer cycles. As my preschooler has already explained for us, when a female menstruates, her uterine lining dissolves and is washed out with some blood. A new uterine lining then builds up, and, if everything is working as it should, the cycle keeps going unless a sperm meets an egg north of that uterus. In one of the few instances of medicine naming something totally logically, "menopause" is the name for when the cycle of menstruation comes to an end. (I suppose they should really call it "meno-end." It's not like menstruation pauses at age 50 and then comes back when you're 80. If it does, go see your doctor.)

During typical puberty, besides the body changing in dramatic ways, an adult sex drive starts to develop in the brain. This means that kids who are going through puberty start to become interested in sex more like we adults are interested in sex. American children today are starting puberty several years earlier on average than they did decades ago. Researchers think this is partly because of better nutrition—good nutrition naturally brings on maturity earlier—although some theorize it also may be because of more toxins existing in our environment; some widely used pesticides known as endocrine disruptors mimic certain sex hormones in our bodies, and the widespread introduction of these chemicals into our environment seems to be causing animals in the wild to have more unusual sex development than in the past.

Regardless of why kids today are going through puberty at younger ages than they used to, this is a problem because their brains are *mostly* still developing along the slower pathway evolution designed, which means they are developing adult sexual urges relatively earlier but not developing good adult decision-making capacity any earlier. Think of it as akin to nature deciding to let kids drive at 10 years of age just because they're tall enough to see over the steering wheel. It's not a great situation.

This is all the more reason we have to talk to our kids about sex—because, on average, children's bodies are maturing earlier than they used to, and sometimes earlier than their brains are really ready for. That's why, now more than ever, we've gotta give those brains a leg up, before the legs go up.

Okay, so let's go over a few concrete examples of talking to your children about sex development and sex difference using normative (generally not helpful) versus descriptive (generally better) language:

Imagine your fifth-grade daughter says to you about a girl in her class, "Alisha is getting *huge* boobs!" A poor, normative (judgmental) answer might look like this:

"Well, her parents feed her so much junk food, of course she's getting huge boobs, and huge all over. It's a shame to see a girl so young be facing such a thing."

A much better, descriptive response would look like this: "Most girls start to develop bigger breasts when they start to go into puberty. Puberty is what changes your body from being childlike to being adult. Children go into puberty at different ages. You're not in puberty yet, but we can expect that you will be within a few years, and then your breasts will grow, too. And your period will probably start then, too. Lots of body-part sizes and shapes and colors vary from person to person. Do you think the other children might be making Alisha feel at all uncomfortable about her body?" (Listen.) "Do you have some questions about how your body is developing or is going to develop?"

Another example: Imagine your young son is digging through his sister's backpack and finds a tampon. He asks you what it is. A poor, judgmental, evasive answer would be: "That's not for boys, and you should not be digging in your sister's backpack! Put it back, and go feed the cat."

A better, descriptive answer would be: "That's called a tampon. It's used when a girl or woman is menstruating as a way to deal with the blood that comes out of her vagina during menstruation. It's basically like an absorbent chunk of cotton. A woman will put it in and keep it in her vagina for a few hours and then take it out, wrap it up in toilet paper, and dispose of it in the garbage. She'll then use a new one until her period ends. Sometimes girls or women use absorbent pads in their underwear instead of a tampon. Those are called sanitary napkins or maxipads."

Take a clean tampon out of its wrapping and show him what it looks like. Answer questions calmly, and then when the conversation naturally draws to a close, move on to the next topic of discussion. (That might include not going through his sister's backpack if that's her private space, because it isn't very considerate to go through people's private spaces if they don't want you to.)

Another example: Imagine your young daughter asks you where she came from since you (her biological mother) and your wife have never talked about her biological father. She knows from school that for conception to happen, the egg from a woman has to meet a sperm from a man.

Evading her questions about this could signal that you are somehow ashamed of her conception—that you are ashamed of how she came into the world. So, instead, approach the conversation honestly and descriptively: "Your mama and I decided to have children, and we talked it over and decided I would be the one to carry you. Of course, we needed a sperm to meet my egg to make you, and women make only eggs, not sperm. So we went to a medical place called a fertility clinic, and we used a tube of semen from a man called a sperm donor. A sperm donor is a man who helps women out by providing sperm so the women can have children if they want to but they don't have another way to get healthy sperm. We don't know the man who donated the semen, so he's what we call an anonymous sperm donor. Your mama and I had help from the clinic putting the semen in me at the time of the month when I was making an egg. We did this three times, because the first two times I didn't get pregnant, but on the third try, I got pregnant with you. Then you grew up in me to become a baby, and you were born. This isn't the way everyone becomes parents—most times, children are conceived because a man and a woman have sexual intercourse by the man putting his penis in the woman's vagina—but it worked for us, and we are so glad you are in our lives as a result. Do you have questions about this?"

Getting the hang of it? Yes, some of this is *terrifying*. But remember that the terror is part of your natural desire to protect children...and then remind yourself that your children are ultimately best protected by knowing the truth about the world. So you have to be brave.

Okay, now let's talk about gender—how we *feel* in terms of our identity.

PART 4

THE BASICS OF GENDER

Remember that old nursery rhyme that said that little boys are made of "snips and snails and puppy dogs' tails" and girls are made of "sugar and spice and everything nice"? Yeah, right. In the previous section, I explained what kids are *really* made of in terms of their biology. Now let's talk about the *social* side of the sexes, namely gender identities. Spoiler: Gender identity turns out to be easily as complicated as sex.

Because most human beings arrive in the world appearing to be either the left-gutter or right-gutter sex types, most human cultures have two associated gender roles: girl/woman and boy/man. Children are usually assigned one of these two genders at birth after a look at the genitals.

Most children have expectations about their genders stamped on them by adults as soon as they are born. In fact, with prenatal testing for sex, nowadays expectations start getting slapped onto our offspring even before they are born. Because we have these nutty ideas about boys being made of puppy dogs' tails and girls being made of sugar and spice, we assign babies names, room decorations, bedding, and clothing according to ideas about what is "right for a boy" or "right for a girl." This is so common that it can be quite challenging for parents to find gender-neutral products. I went crazy trying to find brightly colored clothes for my baby boy that weren't decorated with bows meant to signal the baby was a girl.

Apparently baby boys weren't supposed to wear happy, bright colors like orange and yellow; they were restricted to dark, dull colors in my town's stores.

Why do cultures want you to gender-identify your baby for everybody? That way they can make sure everyone is *on the job* of teaching boys to stop crying and teaching girls to stop being interested in engineering. Plus, gendering sells a lot of stuff. Gender is really good for the economy. (Not kidding.)

But are genders just kids growing into our adult expectations as they relate to sex biology? Is gender about *nurture*? Or is gender *natural*? Do boys naturally like swords and girls naturally like dolls, even without adult expectations being slapped on them?

Parents will tell you that it sure *seems* like children's gendered interests emerge very early without any parental encouragement. Clinical psychological studies and cross-cultural anthropology suggest that, in fact, *nature* may have a lot to do with gendered interests—that is, most young girls may like to do "girl things" in part because of female biological sex development, and most young boys may like to do "boy things" in part because of male biological sex development.

Some pediatricians have told me that if you want to see if a baby has the visual and mental capacity to track something visually, it works best to move a face over baby girls' visual field and move a light over baby boys'—they say that that's how early sex difference becomes evident in terms of gender-different behaviors. Girls go for the face; boys go for the light.

Studies of nonhuman primates (monkeys) seem to confirm that male versus female biological sex development does matter toward the development of male-typical versus female-typical interests and behaviors in many primates. That suggests inborn sex biology probably matters in humans, too.

In several studies, researchers gave young monkeys two kinds of toys: wheeled trucks and plush toys (stuffed animals). The young male monkeys were disproportionately interested in the wheeled trucks, and the females in the plush toys, though on average the female monkeys have more varied interests than the males. In humans, in general, males also exhibit more narrowed interests while females exhibit more varied interests.

I remember that when my son was about six, I was reading one of these monkey-toy studies for work at the breakfast table, and I was telling my son about it. I asked him if he wanted to see the picture that came with the article. It was of a monkey holding one of the trucks. As soon as I showed the photo to my son, he fixated on that toy and asked me very intensely, "What kind of truck do you think that is?" I cracked up and dropped a note to the researchers about my little male monkey.

We could assume my son *learned* from me that he's supposed to be fixated on trucks—that his "boy" interest was a product of six years of *nurture*. There's no doubt that by the age of six, he had gotten many of the messages boys are "supposed" to get: You can't like pink, you should buck up when you're hurt, you should want to be a firefighter and not a ballerina. But, even though culture is pretty pushy (even really nasty sometimes) about gender roles, I think the evidence is pretty good that "gendered" interests have a biological component to them—that they are, in fact, partly about *nature*. The evidence comes in part from studies of kids born with differences of sex development. Researchers find some relationships between the levels of sex hormones your brain was exposed to in the womb and your later interests and behaviors.

That said, again, it is very clear that adults reinforce gendered behavior they see as "appropriate" and discourage behavior they see as "wrong." This has been shown in studies where adults are given human babies who are cross-dressed. The adults do things like become more impatient with "boys" who are crying and try to engage the "girl" babies with "girl" toys.

My husband and I witnessed how differently a baby will be treated if he's perceived as a girl rather than a boy when, one day, we cross-dressed our baby boy and took him out in public. We didn't do it on purpose. We had to go to the mall one day to get holiday presents, and we were totally out of clean socks for the baby. I took my smallest pair of socks, which happened to be bright pink, and put those on him. At the mall, we plunked him in his stroller without shoes—he wasn't walking yet, so why bother with shoes?—and we started wandering the mall.

While we hadn't realized people had been addressing our son specifically as a boy previously, at the mall, it immediately became clear to us that people talk differently to babies they think are girls. At one store, while I was looking for a gift for my mom, a woman came up and started cooing at our son, saying, "Isn't she so pretty! Look at how pretty her eyes are!" My husband and I started glancing at each other. We were simultaneously wondering if it is rude to let someone belabor under a misperception about a baby's gender. Finally, I said to the woman:

"Actually, he's a boy."

She suddenly turned into the human equivalent of a lit bottle rocket.

"Oh!" she stammered, turning bright red. "Well, it's okay for a boy to wear pink, right? I mean, I mean, my husband picked out carpet for our bedroom and he picked out *pink*. That's okay, right? Right?"

We just stared at her, not sure what to say. She fled into the mall like there was an active shooter. At that, my husband, who generally hates mall shopping, turned to me and said, "Let's do this every weekend!"

Obviously children learn about what they are supposed to be like from the way adults treat them, and part of what we do is treat them differently if we think they are one gender rather than the other. Imitating adults, many children will also enforce cultural gender norms, including with siblings. Little girls seem to be especially interested in serving with the gender police. My young son and I used to paint our toenails the same color, and I remember how much this freaked out one eight-year-old girl at the school bus stop. "Nail polish is a *girl* thing," she scolded my kindergarten son, whose sandals revealed the pink polish on his toes.

Just being his usual logical self, he turned to her and asked, "How can it be a *girl* thing if I'm a *boy*?"

"Good point," I observed blandly.

The girl ran off to scream about this to her mother, who later wondered aloud to me when and why her daughter had become a gender-policer.

Whatever third-graders will tell you, genders are actually a lot like sex. Yes, there are *technically* two categories, but in reality they vary a *lot*. And these variations are not perfectly mapped onto sex development. A lot of times, the variations don't mean anything other than that a child has not yet been fully indoctrinated into our somewhat bizarre cultural systems. In spite of what the toy aisles at the store indicate, in practice, "gendered" interests and behaviors vary a lot in biologically typical boys and biologically typical girls. And plenty of children born with intersex conditions are actually gender-typical in terms of their boy or girl behaviors. Genders aren't simple!

Some children show a strong inclination toward the gendered interests and behaviors of the "opposite" gender of the one they were assigned to at birth. So, some girls are pretty consistently boyish from early on, and some boys pretty consistently girlish from early on. Data from all around the world suggest that boys who are more feminine-typical than the average are more likely than the average to grow up to be gay men. We have less data on girls who are more masculine-typical, but the data we do have suggest they end up all over the place in terms of sexual orientation.

Wait, why am I talking about sexual orientation—being gay or straight or bi—when we are supposed to be talking about gender identities? Because, as it turns out, how a child acts and feels in early childhood in terms of gender can give us clues about how the child might end up in terms of sexual orientation as an adult. Look, I know this is not news to you: Boys who are consistently relatively more girlish in early childhood are much more likely to grow up to be gay men than other boys are. Boys who are consistently relatively more boyish in early childhood are much more likely to grow up to be straight men.

Again, the evidence for this comes from all over the world. In fact, in some traditional cultures, there are "third gender" categories for girlish males. In Samoa, for example, young males who express high interest in feminine dress, female-typical social roles, and girls as playmates are put into the category of "fa'afafine" (pronounced fa-fa-FEE-nay), which means "living in the manner of a woman." They are raised like girls in their society and ultimately play the social roles that women do—including eventually taking men as their lovers. The same kind of third-gender systems exist for feminine males in some traditional cultures in South America, Thailand, Mexico, and elsewhere.

What's going on in these cases is a cultural recognition that a feminine male child is likely to grow up to be more interested in feminine-typical social roles, including having sex with men. These third-gender systems actually culturally "normalize" these males by fitting them into a female-typical role early on.

In America, for many generations, we used a much nastier system of "normalizing" males who behaved in feminine ways and females who behaved in masculine ways. That included mocking, bullying, physical abuse, and in some cases, even invasive medical interventions like shock therapy to try to stop gender-atypical adolescents from growing up to be gender-atypical or gay. While you can, to some extent, change how children behave in terms of their gender through systems of rewards and punishment, the evidence is strong that you cannot redirect a person's internal *feelings* with regard to sexual orientation. Trying to do so can lead to great harm. If your child is gay, the sooner you accept it and let her or him know you're okay with it, the less suffering and potential harm your child will face.

In America as in most of the Western world today, some children whose biological sex and expressed gender seem very much at odds will grow up to be transgender adults. Transgender just means that you've rejected the gender assignment given to you at birth because you have found that label doesn't work for you. Identifying as transgender doesn't mean you've had any medical interventions to try to change the biological sex aspects of your body (although you might have, or might later), and it definitely doesn't mean that you were born with an intersex condition or difference of sex development. Remember: Sex is not the same as gender identity. Sex is about biology, and gender is about how you feel. So someone can be transgender even if she or he had nothing unusual in terms of his or her sex development. In fact, most people who are transgender were born typically female or typically male in terms of their sex development.

Again, being transgender just means you've rejected the gender assignment adults gave you at birth, because you feel it doesn't fit you. Some mature transgender people change parts of their sex anatomy through hormones and surgeries, but transgender is about one's identity. That's not to say identity is a trivial matter! Identity is literally the core of our personhood, which is why being denied transition can seriously harm transgender people, and why having access to transition can save their lives by sparing them from brutal physical assaults and suicidal depression. Support can save transgender youth from serious suffering and even death.

As we've moved into a more tolerant culture, children are being subject to less nasty behavior when they act in ways that are relatively uncommon for their gender. So, in general, more boys are being allowed to dress and act "girlish" and more girls are being allowed to dress and act "boyish." This has made gender variation more visible to us all. In the past, for example, few mothers would have felt as comfortable as I have letting my son wear pink toe polish, and few fathers would have felt as comfortable as my mate did when he built our son a toy stove. The norms have loosened up, and we are (thankfully) all spending less time forcing kids into gender norms.

Ironically, the result of this progress is that some parents now think that when their young children act in "cross-gendered" ways or declare themselves to be a boy when they are female or a girl when they are male, that means their children are transgender and in need of medical care to eventually change their sexes with surgeries and hormones. In other words, tolerance of transgender is making parents assume—too quickly, I think—that their young children are transgender when they act in "cross-gendered" ways or say that they are boys when they are girls, or girls when they are boys.

The data actually tell us that most young children who act in gender atypical ways or declare themselves to be the sex opposite of their inborn sex will *not* grow up to be transgender. As I mentioned earlier, in modern Western cultures, young human males who act quite girlish and/or say they are girls will disproportionately grow up to be gay men, not transgender women. Young human females who act quite boyish and/or say they are boys will end up all over the map in terms of sexual orientation, but like the males, most of them will grow to become comfortable with their bodies as they were born. They won't ultimately see the bodies they were born with as wrong and in need of changing, and they won't identify as transgender.

Now, if a child *persists* in what is called gender dysphoria—if the child continues to feel like he or she should have been born with the opposite sex's body—into ages 10, 12, or beyond, then the odds go up that that child *will* grow up to be a transgender adult who wants to change his or her body. In that case, medical intervention to redirect the child's body along the desired puberty, rather than the natural puberty, can be quite helpful to the child or adolescent. Doctors can give hormonal treatments to put off natural puberty, to redirect it along another path if necessary.

So what does all this mean? It means that, with young children, you should pretty much expect a lot of gender variation and gender play. It's part of natural variation and natural exploration, and it's becoming more visible as we calm down about gender roles. Remember, young children also like to play that they are working in various professions, that they are animals, that they are parents. As our culture gets less obsessed with oppressive gender norms—as we get more progressive about men's and women's roles in our world—we're necessarily going to see *more* gender variation and gender play among children.

If your three- or five-year-old daughter says, "I'm a boy," you don't need to run to the doctor. In my opinion, which is based on clinical studies, you should be clear with her that it is fine that she's interested in whatever she's interested in. You should not make her ashamed of her interests, even if the culture around us says "girls don't do that." But you should also not encourage her to think she's going to grow up to have a penis someday.

Am I being a gender-policer when I say that last part? Hmm. I think I'm being pragmatic. We know that most kids that age outgrow stated wishes to be the opposite biological sex or beliefs that they are the opposite biological sex, and all other things being equal, it is best to encourage your child to feel comfortable with his or her body the way it came—to feel good in his or her own skin—whether that's in terms of skin color, nose shape, hair type, missing limbs, genital type, or whatever.

The fact is your biologically female daughter is not going to grow up to have a penis of the kind most boys were born with, no matter how male she feels inside. Even if she grows up to be a transgender man and has the tens of thousands of dollars to pay for a surgically built penis, a surgically built penis is nothing like a natural-born penis in terms of sensation and function. It definitely helps some transgender men to have surgically built penises, but those who have them will also tell you it does not fulfill their wish that they had been born with a male-typical body, because surgery isn't magic. (And genital surgery is definitely not magic, because genitals of all types come naturally magical in terms of sensation, and when you mess with them surgically, you risk messing with those natural magical sensations.)

Some parents think they're being great parents by changing over children's public genders at age three, four, or five. I think they're being way too quick to give in to the old two-gender system. I also think sometimes they're grandstanding to show off what great parents they are, or switching the kid to avoid having to deal with the social awkwardness of a gender-different kid. A better approach is to help children—and others around them—understand that variation in "gendered" interests, behaviors, imaginations, and feelings are acceptable, and to help them understand the reality of the bodies they were born with, so that they come to see their bodies as *normal for them*. All other things being equal, life is much simpler if you can accept and love the body you were born with.

Letting children see gender variation in adults—going ahead and verbally noticing gender variation in adults without mocking or shaming it—helps our children believe that gender variation is normal and acceptable. So, in my household, my husband has for years shamelessly baked in front of our son. Cookies, pies, cakes—you name it. He also grows gorgeous flowers and uses them to create beautiful arrangements for our dining table. Me, I have for years sworn aggressively and gotten into verbal fights with authority figures. ("What's an alpha male?" our young son asked one day. My husband replied, without pause, "Your mother.") We just don't make a big deal of gender-norm violations in our household; we treat them as normal for us, and thereby suggest such supposed violations are in fact normal and acceptable in the world. When our son wanted his toenails painted, we just did it. When he wanted a toy stove, we just built him one. Commenting on these things would have simply given the message "boys don't do that," and we figure boys and girls should be allowed to do whatever is not dangerous as they explore the world. (Plus, with the stove, I figured my son might turn out to be as good a cook as his father, which ultimately would benefit me.)

Again, if a child persists in the feeling that she or he was born with the "wrong" body in terms of sex at age 10 or 12, then we know that the feeling of being transgender (having been assigned a gender identity at birth that doesn't ultimately work well for that person) is more likely to persist, and in that case, parental and clinical support for a possible transgender identity makes sense based on the clinical data. Again, clinicians might use special drugs to try to stop puberty from going in a direction that won't help the child. They can later give hormones to push puberty in the direction the adolescent *does* want. Eventually some will opt for surgeries. Some will opt against medical interventions but will live "gender queer" (mixing up genders or doing without genders) or bi-gendered (shifting between gender roles).

As I've already suggested, medical interventions for people going the transgender route are not trivial—changing over your whole hormonal system is complicated and risky, as is doing any kind of genital surgery— and these interventions can't always give transgender people the bodies they may wish they were born with. Many of the hormonal and surgical interventions can't simply be reversed if someone later changes his or her mind—reversal can be extremely complicated. But if those interventions are really needed for mental and social well-being, then they are really needed. Sometimes they save young people from suicide. That's why more and more insurance systems are recognizing this with payment for these interventions.

In sum, as with sex, the best thing to do with gender issues and your children is to talk with them honestly about reality, including how there's lots of variation in the world, and to recognize that variation is okay, although some people will act like it's not and will get irrational and mean about it. If you chill out about gender, and you teach your children to chill out when it comes to gender, not only will they feel freer to explore the world, not only will they be more tolerant, but they will also get to have that warm, fuzzy feeling of being morally superior to jerks and morons who are overly uptight.

So why don't I advocate raising children without any gender? Why don't I recommend not calling any child a boy or girl until he or she lets us know what is preferred? Part of the reason is, again, pragmatic: The world is set up (mostly) to be divided into only two genders, and not giving your kid a path to try living in one of them early on is just setting him or her up for a lot of potential pain, so much that it strikes me as cruel.

But another reason I don't advocate raising children without gender is this: *Gender is partly about pleasure. And pleasure is good.* Yes, a lot of times gender norms are oppressive and awful. But for many of us, there's a lot of joy in gender—in belonging to a gendered sports league or club, in enjoying the similarities or differences between your child's gender and your own. And the truth is that gender, historically speaking, came out of sex, which exists because of sexuality, which is about pleasure (and babies).

So fighting gender to the point of trying to totally get rid of gender divisions and labels is not only fighting millions of years of evolution—you can do it, but man, it's a *job*—it's also denying the sexual pleasure built into gender. Why deny pleasure when it doesn't always hurt and it often feels good? Gender doesn't have to hurt if we leave room for variation.

We'll talk specifically about sexual pleasure next. But first, let's do a few examples of normative, judgmental language (generally less helpful) versus descriptive language (generally better) when it comes to talking to your children about gender.

Imagine your 10-year-old child says to you, "James is totally into girl things. He wants to hang out with the girls and play with girl toys. Sally says he's a total fag."

An unhelpful, judgmental way to respond to this would be to laugh sarcastically, say, "Sally's probably right," and proceed to gossip about gay kids of your youth. Imagine if it turns out that your child is actually gay and trying to tell you that.

A better way to approach this would be something like this: "The term *fag* is a nasty one. It is usually used as a way to mock people who are gay, and that's not a nice thing to do to people. It is true that sometimes a boy who likes to hang out with girls and who plays with toys that girls generally like will grow up to be a gay man. Sometimes a girl who likes to do so-called boy things will grow up to be a lesbian woman. There were kids like that who I grew up with. It's not always the case that a boy who is into more traditionally feminine things will grow up to be gay, but sometimes, sure, they do. There's nothing wrong with growing up gay *or* straight. But gay kids are often treated badly by the kids around them, and sometimes even by their parents. That hurtful treatment can end up harming the kids who are gay or who are thought to be gay. So why do you think the kids around you are feeling the need to call James names and act like it is a problem if he is gay? What do you think that's about for them?" (Listen.) "How do you think James might feel about all this?"

Another example: Let's say your five-year-old daughter announces to you that she wants to be a fireman, and that her friend said that means she's really a boy.

A rather poor, judgmental way to answer this might be: "Why would you want to be a fireman?! That's a man's job, and besides, you're going to go to college and become a doctor or a scientist like all the successful people in our family."

A better, descriptive way to approach this would be: "It used to be the case that firefighting as a profession was limited to men. Now women are able to go into it too, which is why we usually call them firefighters now instead of firemen. It's a dangerous job and an important one. Wanting to go into a job that used to be only for men doesn't make you a boy. Wanting to go into a profession that requires bravery also doesn't make you a boy. Girls and women can be just as brave as boys and men. Tell me more about why you would like to be a firefighter."

One more example: Your child points to a person on the bus with you and asks, "Is that a man or a woman?"

A typically judgmental way to react is slap the child's hand down and scold him or her for asking. This just leaves many children understandably confused; so much of our world is organized by gender, but they're not allowed to ask what gender someone is?

A better, descriptive way to answer would be: "I'm not sure. Sometimes it can be hard to tell. The thing is, we don't have to know if that person is a man or a woman to deal with them like we deal with everyone else. It can hurt someone's feelings if you get their gender wrong, so it's good to ask politely if for some reason we need to know. But we don't need to know someone's gender to do things like hold the door open for them, let them know they left a glove behind, or whatever we do out of common courtesy. I feel the same curiosity you do when I can't figure out some-one's gender. I'm so used to knowing who is a man and who is a woman without thinking about it. When I can't figure out if someone is a man or a woman, I just remind myself it doesn't have to make me uncomfortable, because everyone is human, and I know how to treat people with common courtesy, so I can manage it."

Okay, let's bring this home by getting to the really challenging bit: human sexual feelings and behaviors.

PART 5

THE BASICS OF SEXUAL FEELINGS AND BEHAVIORS

If human biological sex and human gender are quite varied, which they are, human eroticism is just *nuts*—walnuts, almonds, macadamias, testicles. Pistachios, even.

Statistically speaking, most of us are sort of heterosexual. I say "sort of," because even within "plain vanilla" heterosexuality, there's a ton of variation in terms of what people are really into once they get sexual. The same is true among people who are homosexual and bisexual.

And keep in mind that sexual orientation (what turns you on) is different from sexual behavior (what you actually do), which is also different from sexual identity (what label you choose and/or are given in public).

Although the media tends to talk about three categories of sexual orientation, "gay, straight, and bi" are not the only way to think about human sexual orientation. Most of us are also age-specific in our sexual orientations. So, in terms of age orientation, most of us grow up to be what sex researchers call "teleiophilic"—sexually attracted to adults once we are grown. (So, in a more descriptive sexual orientation system, I would be called a female heterosexual teleiophile.) But some people grow up to be attracted to young children (the name for that sexual orientation is pedophilia) and some adults are attracted to children in the earlier part of puberty (hebephilia). (Don't worry that I'm not saying more about this right now; I'll talk about the importance of consent soon.)

Even beyond our sex- and age-category interests, many of us are attracted to particular kinds of bodies (examples: particular height ranges or ethnic physical features), particular kinds of personalities (outgoing, shy, sporty, bookish), particular kinds of histories (maybe similar to or different from our own), and so on. Then there are various fetishes and kinks, wherein people are into particular objects or body parts (feet, or a special doll), particular material types (latex, leather), relatively uncommon sexual behaviors (exhibitionism), or particular situations (sex in places where you might get "caught").

There is no simple way to explain all this to kids, and *please don't try.* Sexual variety—especially the less common forms of human sexuality—is a topic for grown-ups, *unless* your child specifically asks you about something, in which case you need to talk. The reason I'm telling *you* about it is so that you know that your child may grow up to have sex that doesn't look like the sex you have, and so that you don't lead your children to believe that sex involves only a married man and woman having penile-vaginal intercourse.

What you *do* need is to find several opportunities to explain to your children overtly, as they grow, what most of us found out only in our own explorations: *Human sexuality is mostly about pleasure.* Through natural selection, evolution crafted our sexualities primarily to make sure the species would continue, and continue with some mixing up of the gene pool. No question, sex evolved to be primarily about babies. But, in daily, modern, civilized life, human sexuality is primarily about pleasure.

I honestly didn't fully think about this until my son was in early elementary school. The movie *Juno* had just come out—a film in which a teenage girl, played by Ellen Page, gets accidentally pregnant—and the story apparently went ripping from the sixth grade all the way down to the first graders. As a consequence, my son came home and asked me this:

How can you get accidentally pregnant?

It's not like burning yourself on the stove, he observed to me aloud, where you don't know the stove is on. *How on earth could you have sex without knowing you're having sex? If you don't want a baby, you wouldn't have sex.*

I suddenly realized that I had forgotten to mention to my son that most of the time we are having sex, we are having it because it feels so damned good—we have it for pleasure, not because we want a baby. The result of that pleasure, I explained to him, is that a man and a woman having sex sometimes get all excited and forget to use birth control to prevent the sperm meeting the egg. Sometimes, I explained, birth control also fails. It was, I suggested, like when you get so excited about playing with a rocket that you forget to put your safety glasses on. Or, if the birth control fails, it's like you put your safety glasses on but they broke and you injured your eye even though you had planned to be safe. (We had, in fact, previously discussed birth control, but he didn't seem to remember it, perhaps because when I forgot to tell him that sex is about pleasure, birth control made no sense to him, so he didn't really register it.)

I pointed outside to a squirrel on a tree and further explained: For any sexually reproducing species to continue, there has to be sex to make babies. Evolution has selected for people and other animals who *like sex* when they're grown up, because those who like sex have it, and they go on to make more babies than the animals that don't enjoy sex as much. So, through natural selection over time, evolution has made animals really like sex. Evolution has made sex pleasurable, just like it has made eating pleasurable. Both are about species survival. That's why using our genitals sexually feels good, and that's why we feel sexual attraction as we enter sexual maturity. *Sex feels good.*

I remember he looked so annoyed, like I had forgotten to mention the most important thing about sex. And I had! *It feels really good if you're doing it right.* I had, until then, been so much about the narrative of sex as a mechanical process from which a baby may come that I had completely forgotten to talk about how it involves pleasure.

He then asked me, "Do you and Dad ever have sex for pleasure?" I said yes, that most of the time we have done it, we've done it because it feels really good. I explained to him that we used birth control before we decided to have a baby, and that we stopped when we wanted a baby. I reminded him we were really happy when I got pregnant with him because we felt ready.

He asked me if we still had sex. I blushed and said yes, and said we do it because it feels good, not because we want another child, because we are happy having just him. When you're a grown-up, after puberty kicks in, I explained, it's common to want to have sex when you don't want a baby. Because sex feels good.

I also reminded him that evolution doesn't make children feel the urge to have sexual intercourse, because children are not yet ready to be parents, so nature doesn't make children want sex like adults want sex. When you go into puberty, I explained, you'll develop a special feeling that makes you want to have sex with other people. That's evolution trying to push you to continue the species. You can ignore the push to make babies but still enjoy the pleasure, I said, by using birth control if you're having sex with a girl. If you're having sex with another boy, I said, you don't need birth control, but you still have to think about diseases you can pass between each other and take care of yourself and the person you're having sex with.

He asked me what the sexual urge would feel like. I thought about it, and said to him, "You know how when you have an itch on your back, it feels *so good* when someone scratches it for you? When you are into your puberty, you'll feel a special sexual itch in your whole body that makes you want to have sex with someone you like a lot in that special, sexual way." At first, you'll just want to be around that person, I explained. That's called a crush. Then you might feel the urge to hold hands. Maybe later, you'll have the urge to kiss in a way like sexual partners do. Eventually in your life, when you reach sexual maturity, you'll start to feel the urge to have sex." (Some people never develop the urge; that's called being asexual. We didn't get into that in this conversation.)

I realized, after this conversation, that I had just told him what no one ever explained to me. I had only ever been given the standard talk: "When a man and a woman love each other very much...." In retrospect, that talk made *absolutely no sense* as I started to feel vivid sexual interest during my teen years. I was clearly having sexual feelings for certain men for whom I felt nothing like what love seemed to be. I was clearly having sexual feelings for guys with whom I would *never* want to have a baby. Why would I want to have sex with a guy I did not love?

In fact, the standard, dumb sex talk led me as a teenager to confuse intense sexual interest with love. Disaster! I don't want my son to have that confusion. I also want him to know that sex is so pleasurable, it sometimes leads you to do stupid things, like forget to use protection when you really should, or to have sex with someone with whom you really shouldn't because it's just going to lead to an emotional train wreck. I also want him to enjoy sex without the shame I was taught by my Roman Catholic Polish culture to feel.

Thinking about all this has led me to realize the other thing we forget to tell kids that is so incredibly important: The major question to ask yourself when it comes to sex is *not* "Do I love this person?" but "Do I have this person's meaningful consent?" The corollary also applies: "Do I really want to do this?" ("Do I really want to consent to this?") Meaningful consent is still, frustratingly, rarely taught in sex ed in school. Sex educators sometimes will give kids the definition of sexual assault or of rape—sex without consent—but they rarely talk about what iffy situations and what *positive consent* look like. They rarely talk about the challenge, for example, of saying no to the next "step" in a sexual encounter after you've implicitly said yes to the first few steps by enthusiastically participating.

And that's another important point: You'll hear in the media simplistic accounts of sexual consent simply being the presence of a clear *yes* or clear *no*. But most of the time we are having sex, we are not explicitly asking for *yes* or *no* to be stated. We are instead looking for clues and giving clues. It's great to suggest to your children that they get and give clear verbal consent at every step of a sexual encounter. The reality is that sex often plays out wordlessly, and so they need to be prepared for how to use their words when it is really time.

Moreover, even if a person explicitly says yes, that doesn't mean she really *wants to* say yes—and that's something kids need to understand. Girls and women are particularly taught that they are supposed to take care of and please other people. That can make it very hard for girls and women especially to say no to a potential sexual partner, particularly one who has been nice. No one wants to feel like she can be accused of being a tease.

It can also be very hard to say no to a potential sexual partner if you get something else out of that relationship, like emotional support.

For these reasons, conversations (with your teenagers especially) about sexual consent have to be numerous and detailed. You need to talk about what kinds of feelings you might have that tell you the other person might be saying yes but not feeling it, or that *you* might be saying yes but not feeling it. It would not be unreasonable to tell your son or daughter that you look back and wonder about some encounters you had—about whether you should have decided to stop or slow down when it felt like you and your partner weren't quite in the same mood in terms of what to do with each other. Talk to them about listening to gut feelings. (Also remind them that alcohol and other drugs make it a lot harder to listen to gut feelings and to make decisions well.)

Ideally you should start preparing your children early for respecting themselves and other people sexually. A good way to start modeling consent conversations with a young child is to consistently, respectfully ask permission before you touch his or her body as soon as they are old enough to reply: "May I comb your hair?" "May I help you put your shirt on?" "Would you please hold my hand? I would like to hold yours." If your daughter doesn't want to sit on Uncle Bob's lap, respect her wish so that you make clear to her she doesn't have any obligation—even to loved ones—to experience any unwanted touching. Later, you can refer back to these examples when you start to talk about what sexual consent is—respect for the other person's wishes and your own wishes to be touched or not be touched.

When your child is older (around 12 and up), you can start talking overtly with him or her about sexual consent and what positive consent looks like. You can practice sexual consent with your older child by using an apple or orange as an analogy. Tell your child you're going to practice saying yes and no the way you do during sexual situations: "I really like you, and I'd love it if you'd take my orange. Would you take it?" "I really like you too, but I would like to just talk today, and maybe take your orange another day." "I really enjoy talking with you, but this is not the kind of relationship for me where I want to share fruit with you. I hope you can understand." "I want to share an orange with you but, honestly, I've never had an orange before. How do you feel about trying sharing an orange together? Will you tell me right away if you aren't enjoying it?"

You can talk, then, about good ways to ask for consent and to express that you do want or don't want sexual contact. You can also observe verbally to your child that people in stable relationships often express physical affection without asking—so family members will often reach out to hold hands without any discussion—but that people who don't know each other well often err on the side of less touching and more asking.

Again, it's a good idea to start setting up the context for talking about consent by talking about respecting other people's bodies in terms of whether they want to be touched. Earlier than you want, your child will hear the word *rape,* and you will need to explain that *rape* is the word for when someone touches you in a sexual way—touches your genitals or touches you with their genitals—against your will. Explaining this helps a child understand inappropriate touching. Having already talked about the importance of respecting people's wishes with regard to being touched in other ways will make it all make more sense and be less shocking.

Let me tell you, once you come to these realizations fully—that sex is mostly about pleasure, and that the biggest question in sex isn't whether there's true love but whether there's true consent—it changes how you talk to your children about sex. You start talking in a way that really prepares them to make better decisions. You start teaching them respect for their bodies, and teaching them how to value bodily pleasure in reasonable moderation, as with eating. And so you can teach them, as they get older, to grow up to enjoy sex, relatively safely, without the shame so many of us were taught to feel.

Realizing sexuality is primarily about pleasure and consent also changes how you think about your *own* sex life, because it helps you shed all the shame that we are taught to feel about nonprocreative sex and sexual desire. And having a positive attitude toward your own sex life will give you strength as you teach your children how to have a positive attitude toward theirs. Researchers call this approach "sex positive," in contrast to the "sex negative" messages many of us grew up with.

So, okay, what else do you need to know about human sexuality that they might not have taught you in school? There's enough to fill a dozen books, at least, but here are some key points that might help you get the, um, general feel:

Sex and love: These are definitely not the same thing, but having sex with someone often comes with emotional consequences. There are some people (more commonly males than females) who can have casual sex with no emotional consequences. But particularly for people just getting into their sex lives, sex can get quite entangled with emotions.

A number of teenagers have told me that this is something they wish someone told them before they started getting sexual, because even though they were ready to prevent disease and pregnancy, they weren't prepared for the emotional complications of sex, including how they and their partners often left the encounter feeling differently about it. It's worth explaining to kids why a lot of the sex adults have, they have within the context of long-term relationships: because sex and romantic love are related a lot of the time, although not always, and because sex can bring complicated emotions. Sex is usually better when you trust the other person, and that trust is often easier to achieve in the context of an ongoing relationship, even if it is a "friends with benefits" kind of relationship (in which you are friends who choose to have sex sometimes).

Masturbation: It's normal for everybody, including for people in happy sexual partnerships. (A lot of people use masturbation in happy sexual partnerships to deal with unequal libidos—which are very common—but a lot of people in happy sexual partnerships also do it simply because it feels good as one form of sex.) There's nothing inherently dangerous about masturbation, although you can cause yourself problems if you do extreme things to your body parts (duh). It's common for prepubertal children to touch themselves, even if they don't yet have the equipment to reach orgasm. We do it because it feels good, and—yay!—it's quite easy to get your own consent and impossible to get yourself accidentally pregnant. (There is no type of intersex condition in which you can produce both viable egg and viable sperm, in case you're wondering.)

Disease prevention: When mucous membranes (the soft, wet tissue on the inside of the mouth, the inside of the vagina, etc.) are involved in touching body-to-body, the risk of disease transmission goes up. When there's an exchange of bodily fluid (spit, ejaculate, blood, vaginal moisture), the risk goes up more.

Barrier protection, such as condoms and dental dams, can help prevent transmission of disease by quite a lot. Many sexually transmitted diseases (like chlamydia) are curable, and all sexually transmitted infections are best treated as soon as possible, before complications may set in. Some sexually transmitted infections (like herpes and HIV) are not (yet) curable with medicine, although they can be treated in ways that can reduce the harm to you and also reduce the odds you'll transmit it to a partner. Some sexually transmitted diseases (like gonorrhea) are getting harder to treat.

A critical part of consent in sexual relations is telling someone if you have a sexually transmissible infection. Part of being a responsible sex partner is seeking testing and treatment if you have a reason to believe you might be at risk of having a sexually transmissible infection.

A very common sexually transmitted disease is HPV (human papillomavirus). Many of us catch it in our lifetimes, and for some of us, the body will simply fight it off and we'll clear it (and maybe get it again in the future through more sex). For some of us, this virus will lead to the development of genital warts, and in women, it can also lead to cellular changes in the cervix that can become cancerous. The Pap smear, which tests the cervix's cells, is often done during a woman's gynecological exam to make sure her cervix's cells aren't becoming cancerous because of HPV.

While statistically not very many women in America die of cervical cancer because most get Pap smears and are saved before they develop incurable cancer, having your cervix even start to become "dysplastic" (having the wrong kind of cells) is scary and will require medical interventions that take away a chunk of your cervix. Trust me; I've been there—it's no fun and it leads to a lot of worry, so death is not the only thing to fear when it comes to HPV infections or other sexually transmitted infections. In both men and women, HPV can also sometimes lead to anal and throat cancers, which can be deadly.

Good news! The HPV vaccine, which currently involves a series of three shots over six months, protects against several of the most common strains of HPV. The data suggests it's completely safe for the great, great majority of people who get it, and that it is effective in reducing risk of genital warts and HPV-related cancer. My advice would be to help your child decide, around the age of 11 or 12, if she or he wants to get it. It's a good way to have a conversation about sex, safety, and responsibility to yourself and others, and a great way to signal to your child that you know she or he is going to have sex. (Signaling that makes it easier for them to talk to you about it.)

If you yourself haven't already gotten the vaccine, you could do it at the same time as your child, or in advance of your child if your child is young, so that you can tell him or her later that you got it. Even if you're in a monogamous relationship, that relationship could end through death or splitting up, and you might want to have sex with someone else, so the vaccine is a good idea. Your insurance company might not pay for it if, like me, you get it when you're considered "too old" for medicine to worry about—namely over the age of 26. I paid for it myself and let my son know I was getting it and why I thought he should get it. Many vaccines need to be administered before your child is anywhere near old enough to discuss them and agree to them, but the HPV vaccine is for a sexually transmitted disease specifically, so it can wait until your child is ready to start making decisions that are sexuality-related. The safest approach is to get the vaccine before you start having sex. Since the full vaccination takes six months, and when an adolescent will start having sex is hard to predict, it's a good idea to do the vaccination well in advance of when an adolescent might have sex.

Types of sexual contact: Some people like to give *and* receive sex that is oral, anal, vaginal, or manual (using the hand). Some people like to give and *not get*, or get and *not give*, oral, anal, vaginal, or anal. A lot of sexual excitement comes from context (who you're with, where you are, what's going on in the relationship, how tired or awake you are, etc.). A lot of us get excited when we know we are making our partners excited. That's why, say, giving oral sex can be very exciting even though the giver won't typically get an orgasm.

The prostate: They are definitely not going to tell you this in sex ed: Males can get a bonus from receiving anal sex. A male's prostate sits next to his rectum a couple of inches in, so rubbing his rectum a couple of inches inside can stimulate his prostate and cause him pretty intense sexual feelings. A common myth is that a guy who wants to receive anal stimulation is gay, and another common myth is that all gay guys want anal stimulation. Some straight men like prostate stimulation, and some gay men don't want to receive anal. The desire for anal sex or prostate stimulation has nothing to do with sexual orientation—whether you are straight or gay or bi. (To reach orgasm with ejaculation, the great majority of men will also need direct penile stimulation—rubbing against a hand, inside a vagina, or whatever—but rubbing the prostate at the same time will often enhance a man's orgasm.)

Women don't have prostates, and while I've seen claims of women regularly reaching orgasm from anal sex with no clitoral stimulation, I'm skeptical that this can happen for most women. Although the nerves are definitely interrelated, most women cannot reach orgasm without direct clitoral stimulation. But, like I said, there are nerve connections down there, just as there are hormonal feedback loops that can occur between the nipples and the genitals, and, hell, it's all connected, so you never know. Challenging science through personal experimentation can be fun! (Just get consent.)

The clitoris: Remember, the clitoris is basically the penis in terms of development, except that it has way more nerves packed into a tiny space. Just as most men can't reach orgasm without direct penile stimulation (rubbing), most women can't reach orgasm without direct clitoral stimulation (rubbing or vibrating). We women are, however, taught to *pretend* that we can orgasm just from penile-vaginal intercourse. In fact, in movies, simultaneous orgasm achieved via mere penile-vaginal intercourse is often used as the sign of true love. I think true love is signified by cleaning out the refrigerator without being asked. And I think faking orgasms is a very poor long-term strategy, so it is best not to force a woman to pretend she is reaching orgasm just through intercourse. Keep in mind also that the clitoris is much more sensitive than the penis in terms of touch; touching it too intensely can hurt, as is also true with a penis.

Vaginal sex can feel *so good* to a female because not only does the vagina have a lot of sexual nerves, pushing something—a penis, a finger, a dildo—into a vagina can indirectly stimulate the *internal* part of the clitoris that wraps around the vaginal wall. That's usually what we mean when we talk about "the G-spot." But, again, keep in mind that most girls and women cannot reach orgasm without direct stimulation of the *external* clitoris, the nervy bit on the outside that is most readily available to touch.

Many men think women always masturbate by inserting dildos shaped like penises into their vaginas—and many straight people think that is how lesbians have sex—but many of us women masturbate or have sex with each other using only external stimulation, because the clitoris is where the action really is in terms of orgasm for women. Sigmund Freud tried to claim that women who wanted clitoral stimulation were sexually and psychologically immature, and that psychologically mature women would only want vaginal stimulation. Freud was a sexist pig in this regard, and he did a lot of damage to women and their relationships through this crazy idea that adult women shouldn't want clitoral stimulation.

Gay sex: How do gay people have sex? The same way straight people do: They rub, they lick, they insert, depending on what they are into individually. They do what feels good. The difference is that, because they aren't working with "penis + vagina," they aren't limited by cultural norms that say *that* is what sex is. (That isn't what sex is. A much better definition of sex is that which can feel good sexually.)

Origins of our sexual orientation: We don't really know why some of us grow up straight, some bi, some gay, some pedophilic, some into leather, etc. We don't have a good sense of how human sexuality development works. There have been plenty of theories, and there is some data now suggesting that some men are predisposed to be gay because of having particular genes, and some are likely gay because their mothers had lots of sons in their wombs. (That's called the fraternal birth order effect. You'll have to look it up if you want to know more, because I don't have space to explain here.) For both males and females, the hormone levels in our brains prior to birth seem to matter to some degree in terms of what sexual orientations we end up with. And it looks like sexual interests are set pretty early in life, if not before we are born.

It's possible that for some people, sexual orientation is set very early in life (maybe even in the womb), and that for others, there's flexibility built in, so that it can vary over the courses of our lives. The evidence seems to suggest that, in terms of sexual orientation (as with early childhood toy interest), biological males on average have more narrow, specific sexual interests, and biological females on average have broader sexual interests.

Some adults with fetishes report "knowing" when their sexual fetish developed. They remember a particular instance of sexual awakening tied to their fetish. For example, some people who are sexually aroused by wearing diapers remember a moment when they were forced to wear a diaper and became sexually aroused. We don't know if that's where fetishes come from—particular incidents in childhood—but I do think it is good reason not to expose young children to a lot of potentially odd sexual cues. I think it is absolutely a bad idea, for example, to let children see sexualized rape scenes in movies; we don't know why some men grow up to be primarily aroused by rape, but if there's any chance that is preventable, then let's try to prevent it by not leading children to believe rape is a sexually exciting, normal event. There's nothing inherently wrong with fetishes if they are pleasurable and *involve consent*, but some fetishes can be hard to satisfy in real life, and all other things being equal, your children's lives will be simpler if they develop sexualities that are easier to satisfy. Being open with children about the reality of sex does *not* mean purposefully exposing them to adult sexuality, like pornography. Children do have a right to childhood, and part of respecting them is not treating them as if they are ready for full-blown adult sexuality.

Childhood sexual abuse: Studies suggest that pedophilia (sexual interest in prepubertal children) and hebephilia (sexual interest in pubescent children) are extremely rare as sexual orientations in women and not as rare in men as we would hope. These sexual orientations seem generally to be set relatively early (by the teenage years), as with other orientations, and they do not seem to be changeable. Although many pedophiles say they were sexually abused as children, there is no evidence that sexual abuse of children causes the development of pedophilic orientation in the child abused.

Clinicians can *reduce* the sexual drives of men who are pedophilic and hebephilic, but, unfortunately, they cannot make them not have these feelings. Pedophilia and hebephilia are orientations, and orientations are not crimes. But when these orientations are acted upon, the *acts are crimes*, because children are not capable of consent to sexual relations with adults.

Pedophilic and hebephilic men most often pick as their victims children who are known to them. They tend to be people the parents and the children trust. Be aware that your child is much more likely to be sexually abused by a friendly coach, religious leader, teacher, family friend, or relative than a creepy stranger, which is part of why children have trouble making sense of it and reporting it, and why they are often not heard or believed when they do try to tell someone.

So, let's talk about consent again. Sure, some pedophiles may be "born that way," but while how they *feel* is not under their control, how they act sexually *is* under their control. Again, children are not mature enough to consent to sexual relations with adults, nor is it good for them to become the sexual playthings of adults, even if having their genitals touched may sometimes feel good to some children. One reason it is important to talk to children about sex is so that they understand early that they can talk to you about it. Children who are well educated about sex are almost assuredly more likely to report to you if they are being touched sexually by someone else. (As a reminder, in Part 2, I explained how to talk with children about telling you if someone inappropriately touches them. "When you're not yet sexually mature—before you grow into an adult—these are the only reasons an adult should touch your genitals: to help you with bodily needs and health. If an adult tries to touch your genitals for other reasons, or wants you to touch theirs, that's not okay because that's not something for children. It's like how young children should not be offered cigarettes or race cars to test-drive. That is stuff for adults. If that happens, please tell me right away and I'll help you with it.")

Why aren't we all plain-vanilla heterosexual? When you think at the simplest level, it seems like evolution should have made sure we'd all be born straight and that all men and all women would want only penile-vaginal intercourse with only adults. That's what would seem to lead to the most reproductive success for the species. Instead, for reasons we don't yet understand, the evolution of our species has left us very varied in our sexual orientations and behaviors.

This is probably the case because variety ultimately makes a species stronger—it makes species more ready to adapt to changing environments—even when sexual variety means that not every individual will be born to be as biologically successful in terms of reproduction as he or she might have otherwise been. And keep in mind that, in terms of evolution, "reproductive success" in a family group doesn't always mean each offspring has lots of offspring. There's some evidence that having the occasional gay child be born into a family might ultimately help a family succeed more overall in terms of reproduction, because gay adults often end up giving over resources to nieces and nephews, which concentrates resources in a family rather than spreading them too thin. (This is called the "helper at the nest" phenomenon by biologists.)

But whatever the reason we have sexual variation in the human population, it's again important to remember that in practice, sexuality today, in our modern, civilized world, should be primarily about pleasure and consent. Fuck evolution! (So long as you have evolution's consent.) Repeat after me, ad nauseum: *Sex is about pleasure and consent.*

Well, then—orgasms? Multiple orgasms? Wet dreams? Female ejaculation? What can I say. Again, we vary, and a lot of how we vary is poorly understood in terms of the science. Our generally sexually repressive culture has opted to fund very little sex research. So you'll have to go do your own. Wink, wink.

As far as talking to your kids is concerned, the key lessons to pass on are that sexual desire and sexual relations are natural for mature animals, including humans; that sexuality is something to think about in terms of pleasure and responsibility; and that consent is the core element of responsibility.

Here are a couple more examples of how to answer sexual (or implied-sexuality) questions descriptively:

Say your child says to you, "Kelly Jones doesn't look like her parents at all. She looks Asian, but her parents look white. How can two white people have an Asian child when they have sex?" A good descriptive answer would be: "I'm guessing Kelly is adopted, which means she was conceived by and borne by a woman who is someone other than Mrs. Jones, Kelly's mom. People adopt children for all sorts of reasons. Lots of grown-ups we know were adopted by their parents. [Name some if those adults are "out" about their adoption status.] It's one of the many ways people make families when they want to have children." If your child asks as a follow-up, "So the sperm and egg that made Kelly didn't come from Mr. and Mrs. Jones?," you could answer, "That would be my guess based on having observed the same thing as you, but I don't know for sure. It could be that one of Kelly's parents is her biological parent and the other is a step-parent, and her other biological parent was Asian. Anyway, it might seem like an interesting question to us, but the most important thing for Kelly is that we recognize that Mr. and Mrs. Jones are really her parents now, just like I am really your parent now."

If your child asks you why Kelly would have been given up by a birth mother, you could answer, "Sometimes women place children with adoptive parents because they aren't in a position to raise the children themselves. The birth mother might not have enough social support, for example, or she might be young and wanting to finish school before she raises children herself. Sometimes women give children to adoptive parents because they want to help specifically those parents have a child. There are lots of different ways children come into families. Some, for example, have parents who divorced and then remarried, and that means sometimes they have three or four parents raising them. Families vary in how they come to be. Our family's experience isn't the only way you can have a family."

Now pretend your child asks you, "I heard someone talking about oral sex. What is oral sex?" A good way to answer would be something like this: "When we talk about people having sex, we mean when two adults touch each other in ways that make them sexually excited. It's a kind of feeling you will know after your body sexually matures. A lot of sex between two people involves touching genitals to genitals, but there are other ways adults can touch each other that can cause them to have sexual feelings and to feel good sexually. When one person uses their mouth in a way that feels sexual to the other person, that's called oral sex."

If your child then asks you if kissing is oral sex, you could say: "Most of the kissing people do with each other is not sexual. It's simply affectionate—it shows that you appreciate the other person. When I kiss you, that's an affectionate kiss. When you kiss your puppy, that's you giving the puppy a sign of affection. Sometimes two adults who are in a sexual relationship will kiss in a longer way, with their mouths open more, and that is a kind of sexual kiss because it causes sexual excitement for them. We don't usually call that oral sex, though. What we call oral sex is when a grown-up uses their mouth to touch their partner's genitals in a way that feels good. When you are sexually mature, you will be ready to explore different sexual body feelings and will find out what feels good for you. Everyone is different in what they like or don't like."

Now imagine your 17-year-old tells you she wants to spend the night camping with a person she clearly has romantic feelings for. You could answer in a normative/judgmental fashion: "No daughter of mine is going to be spending the night sleeping around!"

Better would be the realization that your daughter is going to start having sex someday and to have a conversation that unpacks the elements of what she could be getting into. Tell her you recognize that she might be getting into a sexual situation, and ask her whether she needs any assistance to be prepared to protect herself and her partner from unwanted outcomes like disease transmission and, if the other person is a male, from unwanted pregnancy. Then remind her that sex generally has emotional consequences: "A lot of times sexual encounters can lead to complicated emotional responses, and it isn't uncommon for two people to feel differently about a sexual encounter. It's never a bad idea to talk about how you're feeling before, during, and after sex. Talking can be an important and even exciting part of sex, even if it can feel a little awkward."

Finally, make sure she feels confident about managing consent. "Remember that if you're feeling like things are moving too fast, you can say, 'Let's slow this down a little so I keep feeling good.' You don't owe [name] sex, and [name] doesn't owe you sex, just because you've agreed to go out like this together. Remember you need to keep checking in with how the other person is doing and checking in with yourself. If you sense hesitation on either side, respect that and slow down. Taking care of each other's feelings will keep sex feeling good. Sex isn't about getting to a finish line fast. It's best when it feels good the whole time."

Again, yes, this can be hard. So feel free to tell your child, "I haven't really thought about how to explain this, so give me a minute to think about how to explain this." And just keep reminding yourself that children can actually handle a lot of reality and will trust you if you're honest with them.

PART 6

YOU CAN DO THIS! (AND YOU NEED TO DO THIS)

Children want to know about sex, they need to know about sex, and they deserve to know about sex. So, let's review what we've covered:

While there are definitely patterns in our species, in practice, humans vary a lot in terms of sex development, gendered behaviors, gendered interests, sexual interests, sexual behaviors, etc. It should not be surprising if your child or other people around you are different from the average. Being different from the average is not the same as being unhealthy.

Evolution selected for animals who find sex pleasurable, because those who find it pleasurable will have more babies if there's no birth control. So sex is pleasurable for most of us.

And good news! There *is* birth control! There are also lots of kinds of sex that can't ever get you pregnant! That makes sex even more pleasurable—not having the fear of pregnancy. Even better, we've mostly given up crazy puritanical ideas about sex, such as the notion that masturbating will make you go blind. Sex is historically more pleasurable than it has ever been, even though we have to think more carefully than ever about sexually transmitted infections.

Thus, it makes sense today to think about sex as being primarily about pleasure and responsibility (including being responsible through consent).

Trying to convey these sexual values to children as they grow will help prepare them to feel good about sex and to engage in it responsibly.

Children do well when we lean toward descriptive rather than judgmental language, with sex and almost everything else. Leaning toward the descriptive creates an environment in which your child feels safe to talk with you. (It's also probably easier on you.) Talking about lots of things descriptively makes it easier to talk about sex descriptively.

There is no "The Talk." Thinking you are going to give your kid "The Talk" (a single instance in which you tell them everything) is just setting yourself up for an undereducated child who thinks you're not a safe person to go to with sex questions. Plus, *you're* never going to feel safe talking about sex if you save it all up for one big talk. There is *talking*, throughout a child's life, about sex.

So what should you do?

Listen to yourself when you're talking to or around your child. (And remember, they can hear through solid walls.) *Never* assume your child is too young to know what you're talking about with others. Children understand words long before they know how to use them in sentences. They understand attitudes long before they know how to clearly express them themselves. Start talking to them early as though they are intelligent and capable.

Use the right names for body parts. Don't constantly call your son's penis his wee-wee, for example. Also talk calmly about self-care of sexual anatomy. For example, when your daughter is old enough to take showers, remind her, "Wash your armpits, your face, your vulva—wash everything outside your body, and rinse off the soap well." Tell your toilet-training daughter, "Wipe from the front to the back, because there are some germs in the poop in your anus, and you don't want to get the germs into your vagina or your urethra. So wipe always from the front to the back, and then get a new piece of paper if you need to wipe some more. That will help keep your body healthy."

Signal to your child that sexuality is not shameful but sex is something we tend to keep relatively private—and that we do so because of respect for others so that they are not forced to see or participate in something they might not want to. If your child is touching her genitals around others, say, "That's something we do in private. There are some things we do alone, and you're old enough now to do that alone. So just wait until you're alone."

Find a good child's "atlas of the human body" that has useful drawings and explanations of the different bodily systems. Make sure it includes good drawings and explanations of the male and female systems. Pull the book out at least every three months, and let the child linger on various pages, but especially the reproductive pages. Point out the parts and talk about what the book shows.

Try to listen to the world as your child is listening, to be aware of when things are said or shown that she or he might have questions about. Take opportunities to engage in conversation about what's going on.

Don't be like me—always into long descriptions. Sometimes all a child needs is a short conversation or explanation.

That said, if a conversation with your child got heavy or was maybe too light, or if it was just intense for you, follow up later that day or the next day: "Earlier we talked about that preacher on the corner who was yelling about how gay people are all going to hell. I'm still thinking about it some because it troubled me. Want to talk about it some more with me?"

Know you're going to screw up sometimes in these conversations. Go back and take a redo when that happens. Be honest: "I don't think I really answered your question about my period and why I'm bleeding from my vagina, because I was taught not to talk about it. But we can talk about it. It's a normal part of how my body works. Let's talk about it now, and let's look at the book together."

Try to teach your children about consent by consistently practicing it in nonsexual ways, by honoring their right to control how their bodies are touched, as much as possible, as they grow. When they are old enough to actually respond, ask, "May I comb your hair?" "Are you ready for the hygienist to clean your teeth?" "May I have a hug?" (Don't judge if the child says no when you ask for a hug! Just say, "Okay, thank you for letting me know," and move on in a cheery, nonjudgmental fashion that suggests it is fine to say no to touching.) When your child is older, nearing puberty or starting puberty, start talking openly about sexual consent and consider practicing it with an apple or orange.

If your child has a question and you're not sure of the answer, say, "I have to look that up," and then do that and have the conversation. There's no shame in not knowing everything.

The key to all of this is to be realistic about sex: Your child *will* have it someday, and she or he *will* screw it up sometimes. You did. That's part of life.

If you're worried that talking to your child openly about sex will make him or her have sex earlier and with more abandon, know the opposite is probably true: Children who are well educated about sex and who get realistic sex education appear to be no more likely to have sex early, less likely to be involved in unwanted pregnancies, and more likely to take more care with disease prevention.

Besides, if you've been clear with your child that consensual sex is not shameful, that you understand he or she is going to have sex someday, that it is his or her responsibility to take care of his or her health and the health of partners, then *if* something goes wrong, odds are much better your child will seek your help or the help of someone else promptly.

So far as I can tell, the only risk in this approach to parenting is that, like my husband and me, you will end up with a child who knows way more about sex than his peers do, and even a good deal more than his sex-ed teachers do. But if enough children end up in this position, schools are going to have to catch up with our kids. So I say, go for it.

Get off the shame-pride axis. Go forth and describe. And always remember: Sex is primarily about pleasure and consent. Be happy and be responsible to others.